LEADING

by Example

LEADING
by Example

A PARENTAL GUIDE TO TEACHING AND MODELING CHRISTIAN FAITH AT HOME

DR. TIM TOOTEN, SR.

PRESS

Leading by example
A parental guide to teaching and modeling christian faith at home
by Dr. Tim Tooten, Sr.

Printed in the United States of America
Edited by Xulon Press

ISBN 9781545605318

www.xulonpress.com

TABLE OF CONTENTS

Acknowledgements ix

Dedication xi

Introduction xiii

1. The Prelude 1

2. The Problem 3

3. The Prescription 8

4. The Purpose 13

5. The Potential 19

6. The Project 24

7. The Program 28

8. The Plan 33

9. The Progress 43

10. The Parting Words 48

Appendix

A. Participant Training Session One 51

B. Children's Training Session Two 79

C. Session Pictures 155

Bibliography 157

ACKNOWLEDGEMENTS

There are many people to thank for helping to guide this book project from start to finish. This would not have been possible without the support of Virginia University of Lynchburg and its former President Ralph Reavis. The Dean of the School of Religion, Marshall Mays, lent his support, along with the Director of the School of Religion, James Coleman. I owe a debt of gratitude to my faculty advisor, Charles Shannon, III; Core Two reader, Jerome Lee; Pastor A.C.D. Vaughn of the Sharon Baptist Church; and the faithful support of the members of Harvest Christian Ministries.

Many thanks are also owed to many friends for reading different versions of many parts of this effort. Leslie Wilson of the Maryland State Department of Education assisted me in my attempt to fully understand data and how it related to the doctoral process. Fletcher Jackson and Franklin Lance From Mount Lebanon Baptist Church posed questions about the topic that helped solidify my focus. Furthermore, I thank Ronald J. Valenti, Patricia Fosarelli and Vanessa C. Pyatt, who helped to edit the early and latter versions of this document. We thank everyone involved for their encouragement and assistance.

DEDICATION

This book is dedicated to my wife, Charleen. Thank you for your continuous support during my vital educational years. To my children, Fallon, Taren, and Tim Jr. To my son-in-law, Brian, God-son Charles and grandsons Brian III and Elias Timothy. To my mother, Doris Tooten, and my late father, James. To my mother-in-law Roberta Dawson and her late husband Edward Dawson.

INTRODUCTION

"*Leading by Example* desires to serve as a model of ministry for families, and religious and secular educators, seeking a foundational resource to spiritually equip parents and guardians with the knowledge and attitude needed to model and teach their Christian faith. My own life's journey is reflection of faith modeled in my Sunday school class, my home, and my neighborhood. This book comes along at a time when the headlines are filled with breaking news reports focused on crime in the streets of our cities, suburbs, and rural communities. At the core of concern is the lack of a model of faith and reverence within the home structure. This work is designed to assist parents and guardians in identifying their own faith system and teaching and modeling it in the presence of their children and those with whom they come in contact. The Faith community in which I am a part is being challenged to find ways to put into practice ministries and programs to impact a new generation for Jesus Christ. In this book, I will point out why the Bible remains a clear-cut tool in nurturing children in their faith. I will give step-by-step guidance to ensure that children are exposed to Christian principles at home. In addition, you'll be introduced to specific research drawn from a church-wide project conducted within the walls of my own congregation. I've included highlights of this research project as well as a step-by-step teaching and participant workbook designed to give instructors and learners alike, an opportunity to continue to grow.

CHAPTER ONE

THE PRELUDE

*I*t was the only alarm clock I ever knew. It was loud but effective. There were no buttons to press, just a quick response. The alarm clock that sounded in the Tooten home was the voice of my father, James. His words were short, quick and to the point. He reminded my siblings and I that it was time to get up. It was Sunday morning. In our home there was no question or debate about whether you would attend Sunday school or church.

My father's voice carried with it the same tone as it did every other day of the week, including Saturday when we had to arise to take care of our chores. But there was something different about Sunday. The tone of my father's voice was different—you could say divine. By the second call to wake up, if there was a second, we were up dressed and gathered around the breakfast table. As you can imagine, most of us were still wiping our eyes and yawning. My mother took the lead from there starting the day with devotions.

Not long afterwards we would head out the door and onto the grounds of the Springfield Baptist Church, less than fifty yards away. Once we entered the sanctuary, each of us would head to our prospective classes. My teacher was a kind and saintly woman. She taught the primary class that met in the right hand corner of our church, the side where the sun seemed to shine the brightest. I remember that because the sunrays glared on Mrs. Lillie B. Mitchell's face. From where we sat on the second bench, we had to look just above our Sunday school cards. They were five by seven inches, with a picture covering one side and a short lesson on the other. Mrs. Mitchell would let us take turns reading a line or two and then she'd explain the lesson. Those lessons stayed with me over the years. As a teenager, I taught a Sunday school class at the church and later became the Sunday school superintendent. I had no idea that what I was learning in those early years would become critically important in my Christian development. Simply put, my Christian upbringing stayed with me, somehow branded in my mind and within my heart.

After graduating from high school, I left home to attend college in Tallahassee, Florida. Once I received my degree there was an opportunity in television that moved me out of the State from Florida to Washington, DC, then Huntington, West Virginia, and finally Baltimore, Maryland. By this time, I was married, with two small children. In the midst of relocating and finding a home, our family also visited several churches. We settled on a place of worship that was welcoming to families and especially children, the Shiloh Baptist Church of Edgemere. It was evident that beyond Sunday morning, we worked to create a home environment where the teachings of the Holy Bible were carried out. To do that, my wife and I had to rely on what we learned during those early church and home experiences associated with our upbringing. We enrolled in Bible studies at Shiloh and joined the gospel choir, as did the children who took part in choirs of their own. Later, I was promoted to a leadership role. I was ordained as a deacon and eventually chairman of the deacons' ministry. About a decade later, I received the call to preach. This was a major life shift.

I'd always enjoyed sharing my personal testimony of faith with just about anyone I encountered, but standing behind a pulpit was not on my life list of things to do. I accepted the high calling and received invitations to preach all over the city. I had to stay tuned—there was more to come. Another religious shift was in the midst of taking place. On January 31, 2006, I organized a church fellowship called Harvest Christian Ministries in Baltimore County, Maryland, where I assumed the leadership role of Pastor. It was only then that I understood the real importance of Leading by Example.

CHAPTER TWO

THE PROBLEM

A recent survey of parents, conducted by *Children's Ministry Magazine*, shows that when asked how well the parents in their church are doing when it comes to training their children spiritually, 74.4 percent stated that they need some help, 15.8 percent said they are failing miserably, 9.9 percent said they are doing an adequate job. [1] I believe this is partial, yet powerful enough proof of the need to assist parents and guardians in training their school-aged children at home and beyond an organized weekly learning experience.

I realized in the early months of my ministry, as pastor of Harvest Christian Ministries there was a need to not only preach but also teach basic Bible principles. It was several months into our ministry when we established a primary-aged Sunday school class for children ages three to twelve years. Our teachers were consistent in Spiritually training and motivating our youth. But something was missing. Occasionally, parents would pull me aside, turn their attention toward their children and say "Ask the pastor the same question you asked me." No doubt, I felt really bad for the child. At the same time, this process caused something deep within me to search for answers beyond the Sunday morning experience. I thought there must be a way for parents to help their children understand Christian faith the other six days of the week.

---

[1] Children's Ministry Magazine (accessed March 23, 2009).

There had to be a way for parents to have a more hands-on and day-to-day role in the Christian education of their children. I considered what would be a more efficient method to involve parents and guardians in the teaching process in the sharing of biblical instructions within their homes. I relied, in part, on my experience as a veteran television journalist. I began to take particular notice during my frequent visits to schools and neighborhoods that so many children lacked parental support, the kind of bonds that helped in my own personal development. My suspicions were confirmed in talking with public education experts who have long emphasized the need for a greater level of involvement from parents and guardians within the home.

It is for that reason I turned to the work of Dr. Leslie Walker Wilson. In her book, *Improving Your Elementary School,* Dr. Wilson shed light on a problem already affecting parents and guardians of elementary schoolchildren. Wilson writes that there is constant stress and struggle to find enough time for children. She says many parents are faced with working multiple jobs or dealing with other external pressures. Wilson goes on to say that these struggles do not change the fact that most parents want the best education possible for their children.[2]

I sought to hear from the thousands of children who expressed their own personal challenges and choices.

This came by way of a 2007 adolescent survey, by the Maryland State Department of Education's Student and School Services. It seemed to bear proof of the need for home-based discipleship training. The survey was completed by 33,057 adolescents and represented 12 to 14 percent of the State's enrollment. The survey was administered to samples of sixth, eighth, tenth, twelfth graders in elementary, middle, and high schools in every school system in Maryland. There was an 84 percent overall response rate. The data showed that almost 40 percent of twelfth graders have tried marijuana and 20 percent of tenth graders have used marijuana during the last year. Almost 21 percent of twelfth grade marijuana users started using at age 12 or younger, and a

---

[2] Leslie Walker Wilson, *Improving Your Elementary School,* (New York: Eye on Education, 2007). pg.63.

little more than 38 percent of twelfth grade marijuana users started using at ages 13–14. Almost 62 percent of 6th grade boys and 38 percent of 6th grade girls reported in the survey they had used marijuana and alcohol.[3]

A similar document, the 2005 Maryland Youth Risk Behavior Survey, concluded there was a spike in the use of all other drugs in the 12th grade.[4] Nearly 75 percent of Maryland and nationwide, high school students have tried alcohol at least once.[5] The data also shows that between grades 10 and 12, Maryland high school students showed an increase in the percentage of those who smoked cigarettes in the past 30 days. Even more disturbing was that about 1 in 5 Maryland high school students or nineteen percent carried a weapon in the past 30 days.[6] Another 14.9 percent of Maryland high school students had been involved in a physical fight on school property over the past 12 months.[7]

There are more data that suggested the need for biblically-based intervention in homes within the geographical areas of our church. High-school aged juveniles (ages 14 and older) made up 80 percent of the delinquency cases in 2002; older teens (ages 16 and older) accounted for 42 percent. In comparison, middle school-age juveniles (age 12 and 13) were involved in 16 percent of delinquency cases, while juveniles younger than 12 accounted for 5 percent.[8] In the past three years or more I have witnessed the parental-child challenges, both within my congregation and the mission field.

The problem I am called to address is the need for parents and guardians within Harvest Christian Ministries to become biblically equipped to lay a foundation of Christian discipleship in the lives of their children and those they are responsible for nurturing. As editor of the book *Children's Spirituality: Christian*

---

[3] Maryland Adolescent Survey, Maryland State Department of Education. 2007: http://www.marylandpublicschools.org/NR/rdonlyres/852505C8-7FDB-4E4E-B34E-448A5E2BE8BC/18944/MAS2007FinalReport_revised111808.pdf (accessed on May 30, 2008).

[4] Maryland Youth Risk Behavior Survey, Maryland State Department of Education. 2005: http://www.marylandpublicschools.org. (Accessed on May 30. 2008).

[5] Ibid.

[6] Ibid.

[7] Ibid.

[8] Juvenile Offenders and Victims National Report Series, 2006: http://ojjdp. ncirs.org (accessed on May 30, 2008).

Perspectives, Research, and Applications, Donald Ratcliff shares the thoughts of those who suggest that many congregations offer weak religious education programs, failing to emphasize the importance of parents in faith development. The book further states that many parents do not know what their children are learning in Sunday school, and parents are not given the sense that they are primarily responsible for the faith formation for children.[9] This has not been my personal experience, by and large. In fact, I learned there was a lack of shared responsibility on the part of the Christian community to assist parents and guardians to fully embrace the spiritual nurturing of their children.

I made some additional notes gathered from the findings of Donald Ratcliff's book, in particular, those which pointed to a study by the *Search Institute* of eight-thousand adolescents, whose parents were members of congregations in eleven different Protestant and Catholic denominations. Only 10 percent of these families discussed faith with any degree of regularity, and in 43 percent of the families, faith was never discussed.[10]

The author also believes that adults are not attending to the "whole being" of children and providing them with emotional, intellectual, moral, and spiritual guidance.[11]

I agree with the summation of this author as it relates to the critical role the church, parents, guardians must play in order to reach for the cause of Christ.

Children are God's gifts not only to their parents, but also to the community. They are members of a community from the start, and they play various and complex roles within it. In addition, they will grow up to be not only sons and daughters but also husbands and wives, friends, neighbors, and citizens. Viewing children as gifts of God to the whole community radically challenges common assumptions of them as "property" of parents or "economic burdens" to the community.[12]

---

[9] Donald Ratcliff, Children's *Spirituality, Christian Perspectives, Research and Applications*, (Eugene Oregon: Cascade Books, 2004), p. 43.
[10] Ibid.pg.43.
[11] Ibid.pg.43.
[12] Ibid. pg. 45.

This was an issue that had to be taken seriously; but at the same time, I was convinced that a person must identify where the responsibility ought to be placed as it relates to responding to the Christian educational needs of today's youth. I don't believe that the church can and should bear the burden alone of educating school-aged children. I agree with the assessment of the late Dr. Harold A. Carter, Sr., who shared this insight in his book, *America, Where Are You Going?* Carter stated:

> One wonders whether Christians today have any knowledge of God's purpose and place for the Christian home as a foundational stone in life. Do we have the knowledge that the home has been called to be a place of love, of worship, of instruction in God's word, of obedience to God's word and of evangelism? There has been such a shift of emphasis, from the responsibility that ought to reside in the home, to the arguments about what the school ought to do and the society at large.[13]

Carter was not alone in his observation. George Barna is among the writers, who have recognized the value of having parents and guardians become involved in the life of children, especially in the early learning years. In his book, *Transforming Children into Spiritual Champions: Why Children Should Be Your Church's #1 Priority,* Barna asserts that most churchgoing parents are neither spiritually mature nor spiritually inclined and, therefore, they do not have a sense of urgency or necessity about raising kids to be spiritual champions. Most parents believe that encouraging their children on a regular basis to feel generally positive about their religious experience is as high as they can set the bar. Anything achieved beyond that level is seen as a bonus.[14]

---

[13] Harold A. Carter *"America Where are you Going"* Gateway Press, Inc. Baltimore MD, 1994), pg 23.
[14] George Barna, *Transforming Children into Spiritual Champions: Why children should be your church's #1 priority,* (Regal: Ventura California, 2003), pg.78.

CHAPTER THREE

THE PRESCRIPTION

I believe the church, the body of Christ, must remain as a beacon of hope for the spiritual formation of the family. It's one of the points made by author James C. Perkins in his book, *Building Up Zion's Walls,* in which he observed that the Lord's instructions to parents are explicit. He noted that parents have a duty to teach their children the ways of the Lord in their own homes. Of course, church attendance, Sunday school, children's church, and Christian youth groups all are important. Each has its place in the nurture, development, and socialization of children and teens. But the home makes an indelible mark on them. Perkins went on to say that children learn how to live, and they learn what it means to be connected within a family. They watch parents eat, sleep, talk, laugh, and cry. They watch how parents react to pain and sorrow as well as pleasure and joy.[15]

Scott Cooper provides another insight that helped to shed light on the role of parents and guardians in teaching and modeling Christian discipleship principles. In his book, *God at the Kitchen Table: Teaching Your Religious and Moral Beliefs to Your Children,* Cooper makes the following observation:

---

[15] James C. Perkins, *"Building Up Zion's Walls,"* (Valley Forge PA: Judson Press, 1999), pg.12.

We can offer religious and moral training at home whether we've found a comfortable place within organized religion or not. Religious institutions can't replace the influence of our own beliefs, teachings, and example. If we want our children to pick up on the values that are most important to us, we need to take direct responsibility for teaching and living those values. If we want our kids to have gratitude and reverence for God, we need to express that gratitude and reverence in the home. Organized religion can be helpful, but it can't replace the role of the parent as the primary moral guide and mentor.[16]

In the 2008 book, *Nurturing Children's Spirituality,* edited by Holly Catterson Allen, a number of experts in the field note that children were considered holy gifts from God; their arrival was greeted by their parents and community with much celebration-with a sense of great joy that life was good, for God had blessed the world with another child.[17]

I believe that with such a high value placed upon children, the faith community can no longer expect Church and school settings alone to equip children spiritually for a life of obedience and reverence to God. It will become increasingly necessary to link church and school learning with parents in a home setting, similar to the growing home-school education movement.

As it relates to family, Fordham University professor Robert J. Parmach helps to define family. He states that we gain an enriched sense of what is meant by family by drawing some helpful parameters, a *via negative* of sorts, of what the family is not. He says biology is not necessary for family; neither is common residence, economic status, nor affectionate relationships. Parmach goes on to say that family transcends the legal, geographical, and financial

---

[16] Scott Cooper, *God at the Kitchen Table, Teaching your Religious and Moral beliefs to your children* (Three Rivers Press, New York 2002), pg.5.

[17] Holly Catterson Allen, *"Nurturing Children's Spirituality, Christian Perspectives and Best Practices.* (Eugene, OR: Cascade Books), pg.81.

categories to that of a deep religious dimensionality of living. He says family is not a temporary classification; it persists through time and through intimate interrelationships.[18]

There are a number of other authors whose insight caught my attention as it relates to shaping the family. One is Gabriel Moran. In his book, *Religion and Lifelong Learning,* Moran stated that, "During the history of the colonies and the United States there has been an almost continuous belief that the family has just disintegrated. Actually, the problem is almost the reverse."[19] Moran wrote that the family is such a topic of concern because it has not collapsed and can be seen to sag under the weight of its communal burdens."[20]

The family unit has remained steady by God's providence and that one must be cognizant that Christ has to be at the center of any Christian education model. In his book, *Leadership in Religious Education,* David Arthur Bickimer stated, "In a very real sense Christ is still the leader in any religious education situation. He is still a servant to his modern-day disciples. But he can only be this by and through those he calls to be the servants of the religious education community, today's leaders and would-be-leaders."[21]

It is believed that physical and intellectual nurturing should not begin and end with pre-kindergarten and a high school or college diploma respectively, but become a life-long experience.

The work of author Marcia J. Bunge is worth noting as it relates to the spiritual significance of nurturing children in their faith. In her book, *The Child in Christian Thought*, Bunge shares some of the very insights I've long supported. She says there are five main ways in which the significance of children is underscored in Jesus' teaching and practice. Bunge says first He blessed the children brought to him and taught them that the reign of God belongs to them. He made children models of entering the reign of God. He also made

---

[18] Ibid. pg. 81.
[19] Gabriel Moran, *Education toward Adulthood.* (Paulist Press: New York, 1979), pg.92.
[20] IIbid pg. 93.
[21] David Arthur Bickimer, *Leadership in Religious Education,* (Religious Education Press: Birmingham, Alabama, 1989), pg.47.

children models of greatness in the reign of God. He calls his disciples to welcome little children as He does and turns the service of children into a sign of greatness in the reign of God. He gave the service of children ultimate significance as a way of receiving himself and, by implication, the One who sent him. He was acclaimed by children as the "Son of David."[22] The author also notes that childhood was viewed above all as a training ground for adult life, not as a valuable stage of life itself. This accounts for the greatest stress placed on education.[23]

Author Charles M. Sell who in his book, *Family Ministry: the Enrichment of Family Life through the Church,* lifts up, in part, the role of the Church and pastor to equip parents to pass along the faith. Sell seemed to suggest that the Church is called to do more to help parents watch for the child's questions.

> The Old Testament pattern capitalized on children's curiosity in order to have truth passed on to the next generation: "In the future, when your son asks you, what is the meaning of the stipulations, decrees and laws the Lord our God commanded you tell him..." (Deut. 6:20–21). Parents might easily overlook opportunities to teach, since children's questions are most often posed at the wrong time. The wise mother later goes back to the question her impulsive young son asked her just as she was sliding the hot chicken from the pan to the platter. Wise parents make it a pattern to go to the shelf for the Bible as they do for the encyclopedia when children are searching for answers. [24]

Dr. Ben Carson, Famed Johns Hopkins University neurosurgeon and current United States Secretary of Housing and Urban Development, points to

---

[22] Marcia Bunge, *The Child in Christian Thought,* (Grand Rapids MI: William B. Eerdmans Publishing Company. 2001), pg. 36.

[23] Ibid.

[24] Charles M. Sell, *Family Ministry: The Enrichment of Family Life through the Church,* (Grand Rapids, Michigan: Zondervan Publishing House, 1981), pg.217.

need for parental involvement in the lives of children. In his book, *Take the Risk,* and what he shared with me says, "The most useful weapon we have in this daunting task is the marvelous brain we've each been given. So the first order of business may be for parents to use ours to teach our kids how to use theirs."[25]

---

[25] Ben Carson, *"Take the Risk,"* (Grand Rapids, Michigan: Zondervan, 2008).pg.203.

CHAPTER FOUR

THE PURPOSE

I am convinced that religious education is properly rooted in the sacred texts of Holy Scripture. God, through His prophets, appears adamant about His chosen people receiving a life-changing education, one that could be handed down through future Generations. I believe the faith community is commissioned to evangelize and encourage a new generation of God's people, youth in particular, to adhere to genuine spiritual and moral guidance.

I'll make mention throughout this chapter of Scripture passages from both the Old and New Testament writings of the Holy Bible that bear witness to the fact that it was God's intent for His chosen people to take on the responsibility of nurturing their children in their faith. There is evidence of that charge by way of God's servant Moses in Deuteronomy 6:4–9. Unless otherwise noted. Scripture passages are taken from the New International Version of the Bible.

> Hear, O Israel: The LORD our God, the LORD is one. Love the LORD your God with all your heart and with all your soul and with all your strength. These commandments that I give you today are to be upon your hearts. Impress them on your children. Talk about them when you sit at home and when you walk along the road, when you lie down and when you get up. Tie them as symbols on

your hands and bind them on your foreheads. Write them on the doorframes of your houses and on your gates.[26]

I was drawn to the work of Everett Ferguson, who, in his book *Backgrounds of Early Christianity,* made specific reference to the words of Moses in that same 6th chapter of the book of Deuteronomy. These particular scripture passages are well known in the Jewish faith. Ferguson went on to say that it was the faithful Jew who recited the Shema, not only in the synagogue but daily. The author noted that *Shema* ("Hear") is the opening word of Deuteronomy 6:4 and is the basic confession of Judaism.[27] God would use other leaders to remind His people of the importance of learning specific lessons from history, particularly those which refer to where God brought His people from and the importance of their sharing stories of faith with the next generation. I make reference to Psalms 78:1–6 which appears to illustrate the significance of people of faith to not only hear the Holy Scriptures but to deposit them in the minds and hearts of their children.

O my people, hear my teaching; listen to the words of my mouth. I will open my mouth in parables, I will utter hidden things, things from of old — what we have heard and known, what our fathers have told us. We will not hide them from their children; we will tell the next generation the praiseworthy deeds of the Lord, his power, and the wonders he has done. He decreed statutes for Jacob and established the law in Israel, which he commanded our forefathers to teach their children, so the next generation would know them, even the children yet to be born, and they in turn would tell their children.[28]

---

[26] Deuteronomy 6:4-9 (New International Version).

[27] Everett Ferguson, "Backgrounds of Early Christianity, (Grand Rapid, Michigan: William B. Eerdmans Publishing Company, 1993. pg. 257.

[28] Psalm78:1-6 (New International Version).

It's been my personal experience that when parents commit to teaching their children the value of making sound spiritual decisions, the children are less likely to model the negative influences of their environment. The wisdom writer reinforces the importance of consistent and faith-filled teaching in Proverbs 22:6. Train a child in the way he should go, and when he is old he will not turn from it.[29]

There are countless other examples in Scripture which appear to support the need for parental involvement, among them, the writings of the prophet Joel who made the following observation in Joel in Joel 1:1–3.

> The word of the Lord that came to Joel son of Pethuel. Hear this, you elders; listen, all who live in the land. Has anything like this ever happened in your days or in the days of your forefathers? Tell it to your children, and let your children tell it to their children, and their children to the next generation.[30]

In the book of Acts, persecution and oppression swept the New Testament church and its followers who retreated to their homes to share the truths of the gospel with their families. In Acts 4:23–24, there is evidence of the church's willingness to live for Christ and share the gospel in spite of their present circumstances. I believe they modeled a strong witness to their families and the wider church community by sharing their testimonies.

> On their release, Peter and John went back to their own people and reported all that the chief priests and elders had said to them. When they heard this, they raised their voices together in prayer to God. "Sovereign Lord," they said, "you made the heaven and the earth and the sea, and everything in them.[31]

---

[29] Proverbs 22:6 (New International Version).
[30] Joel 1:1-3 (New International Version).
[31] Acts 4:23-24 (New International Version).

There were also instances within the persecuted church in which there was a display of faith and unity in regards to the New Testament Church, as highlighted in Acts 4:32–33.

> All the believers were one in heart and mind. No one claimed that any of his possessions was his own, but they shared everything they had. With great power the apostles continued to testify to the resurrection of the Lord Jesus, and much grace was upon them all.[32]

Jesus Christ set the example of what it means to place divine value on the lives of children. In Mark 10:13–16, parents recognized the value of having their children blessed by Jesus. However, not everyone viewed this as a positive occasion.

> People were bringing little children to Jesus to have him touch them, but the disciples rebuked them. When Jesus saw this, he was indignant. He said to them, "Let the little children come to me, and do not hinder them, for the kingdom of God belongs to such as these. I tell you the truth, anyone who will not receive the kingdom of God like a little child will never enter it." And he took the children in his arms, put his hands on them and blessed them.[33]

There remained an emphasis on the parental role in the education of children. In Luke 2:45-48, I am made aware of the early childhood and educational training of Jesus Christ.

> When they did not find him, they went back to Jerusalem to look for him. After three days they found him in the temple courts, sitting

---

[32] Acts 4:32-33 (New International Version).
[33] Mark 10:13-16 (New International Version).

among the teachers, listening to them and asking them questions. Everyone who heard him was amazed at his understanding and his answers. When his parents saw him, they were astonished. His mother said to him, "Son, why have you treated us like this? Your father and I have been anxiously searching for you.[34]

The Apostle Paul was able to reflect on his own personal religious upbringing as it relates to a changed life in1 Corinthians 13:11–13.

When I was a child, I talked like a child, I thought like a child, I reasoned like a child. When I became a man, I put childish ways behind me. We see but a poor reflection as in a mirror; then we shall see face to face. Now I know in part; then I shall know fully, even as I am fully known. And now these three remain: faith, hope and love. But the greatest of these is love.[35]

Paul also shared what could be interpreted as the responsibility of children to live out their faith at home and in the world in Ephesians 6:1–4.

Children, obey your parents in the Lord, for this is right. "Honor your father and mother"-which is the first commandment with a promise— "that it may go well with you and that you may enjoy long life on the earth." Fathers, do not exasperate your children; instead, bring them up in the training and instruction of the Lord.[36]

In 2 Timothy 1:5–7, the Apostle Paul reminded Timothy of the value of the spiritual teachings which had been embedded within his own experience.

---

[34] Luke 2:45-48 (New International Version).
[35] 1 Corinthians 13:11-13 (New International Version).
[36] Ephesians 6:1-4 (New International Version).

When I call to remembrance the unfeigned faith that is in thee, which dwelt first in thy grandmother Lois, and thy mother Eunice; and I am persuaded that in thee also. Wherefore I put thee in remembrance that thou stir up the gift of God, which is in thee by the putting on of my hands. For God hath not given us the spirit of fear; but of power, and of love, and of a sound mind.[37]

---

[37] 2 Timothy 1:5-7 (New International Version).

CHAPTER FIVE

THE POTENTIAL

*A*s pastor and founder of Harvest Christian Ministries, I recognized the need to extend the teaching of God's word to school-aged children outside of the Church and beyond the Sunday learning experience. Harvest school-aged children are exposed to a weekly curriculum that helps to meet the physical, spiritual, cognitive and emotional needs of children. Author John M. Perkins sees the role of the church as significant in the restoration of communities, and subsequently the family. Perkins makes this assessment in his book, *Restoring At-Risk Communities: Doing it Together and Doing It Right.*

> The people of God functioning as a church community are the best means of affirming the dignity of the poor and empowering them to meet their own needs. It is practically impossible to do effective holistic ministry apart from the local church. A nurturing community of faith can best provide the thrusts of evangelism, discipleship, spiritual accountability, and relationship by which disciples grow in their walk with God.[38]

---

[38] Perkins, John M. *Restoring At-Risk communities Doing it together and doing it right* Baker Books Grand Rapids, MI 2008), pg.23.

Scottie May, Beth Posterski, Catherine Stonehouse and Linda Cannell continue to make the case of the importance of children's spirituality in their book, *Children Matter: Celebrating Their Place in the Church, Family, and Community*. They suggest that what we know about children in the early Church comes largely from incidents scattered throughout the Gospels and epistles, augmented by what we read about the times in other documents.

> We have glimpses of the childhood of Jesus and of John the Baptist. There are references to children being in the crowds who came to listen to Jesus teach (John 6:9; Matthew 14:21). Of particular interest are the stories about Jesus welcoming children and His teaching about children being role models in the kingdom of God. Some of Jesus' healing miracles involved children. The raising from the dead of Jairus's daughter (Mark 5:21–24, 35–43; Matthew 9:18, 23–26; Luke 8:40–42, 49–56) and the healing of the royal official's son (John 4:46–51) are two such incidents.[39]

There is a need for the 21st century church to embody the spirit and responsibility echoed in the gospels. In order to assume the reins of children's spirituality, the church much continue to be a sanctuary for childhood. I am certain that references like the ones gleaned from Herbert Anderson and Susan B.W. Johnson in their book, *Regarding Children, A New Respect for Childhood and Families,* are worthy of consideration by parents, guardians, church leaders and teachers. They suggest that:

> If a church transforms its attitude toward children in order to be a *sanctuary for childhood,* it will deepen the sacred trust of its access to families. What the church has ordinarily done for children and

---

[39] Scottie May, Beth Posterski, Catherine Stonehouse and Linda Cannell, *Children Matter: Celebrating Their Place in the Church, Family, and Community,* (Grand Rapids, Michigan: Wm, B. Eerdmans Publishing, 2005), pg.89.

families will take on new significance. It will welcome children as full participants in the life of God's people; it will support the vocation of being a parent throughout its ever-changing roles; the formation of faithful children will have new direction and urgency.[40]

And there's this insight shared by a number of respected Christian education professors in Lutheran seminaries. It appears that their discussion in the 2004 publication *The Ministry of Children's Education,* authored by Margaret A. Krych, has the making of a model for the church at-large in ministering specifically to families.

Whatever happens to a child happens to the whole family. Whatever happens to the family also happens to the child. There is much to know about children themselves and the church's ministry with children, but ministry with children must happen within the context of their families. Within their families and their homes, children have most of their physical and emotional needs met, spend a majority of their time and catch the values and priorities of their parents or caregivers.[41]

This project was undertaken with psychological and social considerations. The late Charles Haddon Spurgeon. In his book, *Spiritual Parenting,* Spurgeon shared his passion as it relates to the role of the church in ministering to children.

As soon as a child is capable of being lost, he is capable of being saved. As soon as a child can sin, that child can, if God's grace

---

[40] Herbert Anderson and Susan B. W. Johnson, *Regarding Children, a new perspective for childhood and families* (Louisville, KY: Westminster John Knox Press, 1994), pg.113.

[41] Margaret A. Krych, *The Ministry of Children's Education: Foundations, Contexts, and Practices,* (Minneapolis, MN: Fortress Press, 2004), pg.104.

assists him, believe and receive the word of God. As soon as children can learn evil, be assured that they are competent to learn good under the teaching of the Holy Spirit.[42]

My own parents were consistent in applying their level of biblical training within the home. Furthermore, biblical lessons were modeled during daily life; primarily, the work ethic of my disabled father, who recalled making sacrifices as a fatherless child in his youth during the Great Depression. It was also modeled by my mother, who was raised by her maternal aunt, and subsequently came under the religious tutelage of an uncle, who was also a pastor. Her embedded theology was passed on to her children.

In order for parents and guardians to teach and model their faith, they must be aware of how their child develops. A helpful book for my research is *A Piaget Primer: How a Child Thinks* by authors Dorothy G. Singer and Tracey A. Revenson. They identify four overarching elements that guide development: emotions, maturation, experience, and social interaction. They point out that all four components work together in guiding development and creating enough disequilibrium to motivate learning. Emotions create the feelings that motivate and excite learning. Maturation is the physical growth process. Through differentiation of the nervous system, mental structures develop, and the child becomes capable of great understanding.

Experience is a major catalyst because it's only through exposure to a variety of experiences that children can make discoveries for themselves. Social interactions with other people—especially parents, teachers, and other children—provide those experiences, as well as feedback. The authors say it is important to remember that these four components work together synergistically; for example, the child's mental structures must be developed

---

[42] C.H. Spurgeon *"Spiritual Parenting"* (Whitaker House New Kensington, PA 2003), pg.110.

enough to be able to understand and assimilate the information she is given by parents.[43]

Authors like Patricia Fosarelli shared the importance of integrating physical, social, moral, intellectual and spiritual development. Fosarelli in her book *ASAP: Ages, Stages, and Phases: from Infancy to Adolescence,* suggests:

It is difficult to fully understand people by exploring only one aspect of development, as each aspect influences the others. To know something about an adult, we need to know something about adult levels of development, we need to know about levels of development at younger ages.[44]

Since it is my intent to help parents and guardians of children aged 3 to 12 years, I am particularly drawn to other comments from Fosarelli. She says one of the ways of assisting the learning of pre-teens is to realize that at this age, children love Scripture stories in which mighty deeds are done, whether it's Moses parting the Red Sea or Jesus feeding the multitudes with very little food. Such stories spark children's imagination, and they respond well to them. Use them liberally.[45]

---

[43] Dorothy G. Singer and Tracey A. Revenson, *"A Piaget Primer how a child thinks."* (Penguin Books: New York, 1996), pg.18.

[44] Patricia D. Fosarelli. *A.S.A.P Ages, Stages, and Phases, From Infancy to Adolescence,* (Liguoir MO: Liguori, 2006), pg.1.

[45] Ibid. pg. 75-76.

CHAPTER SIX

THE PROJECT

*I*n an effort to develop an age-appropriate curriculum for members of my church and community, I specifically designed sessions that would address the cognitive, spiritual, emotional, and physical development of children. In doing so, I believe learning was enhanced throughout the educational process established to assist parents and guardians in teaching and modeling their Christian faith with their children at home.

I was drawn to the research of Jean Piaget. In her book, *The Psychology of the Child*, she observed that beyond spoken language, children are influenced by imitation. Piaget says:

> When someone performs in front of a child a gesture the child has just made, the child will repeat the gesture. A little later, the child will imitate any gesture made by the adult, provided that at some time or other this gesture has been performed by the child himself.[46]

From the outside, I believe this is a behavior worthy of noting as parents and guardians lay the foundation for teaching children in the home. And then

---

[46] Jean Piaget and Barbel Inhelder, *"The Psychology of the Child"* (Basicbooks: New York, 2000), pg.55.

I considered the research of Israel Galindo in his book *The Craft of Christian Teaching: Essentials For Becoming a Very Good Teacher.* Galindo believes:

> As Christian teachers we need to use those instructional methods that will most effectively help our learners incorporate the truths of God's self-revelation into their minds and hearts. All methods are not equivalently effective for all teachers: part of the artistry of teaching lies in discovering those strategies most appropriate for you as a teacher, your student, and your lesson.[47]

I took into account the importance of understanding the ways children learn. This led me to the groundbreaking contributions of Howard Gardner in his book, *Frames of Mind, The Theory of Multiple Intelligences.* Gardner seeks to challenge the widely held notion that intelligence is a single general capacity possessed by every individual, to a greater or lesser extent. Gardner pointed out:

> To my mind, a human intellectual competence must entail a set of skills of problem solving—Enabling the individual to resolve genuine problems or difficulties that he or she encounters, when appropriate, to create an effective product—and must also entail the potential for finding or creating new problems—thereby laying the groundwork for the acquisition of new knowledge.[48]

This is how I went about assessing the needs of children, parents and guardians within my own congregation. The participants consisted of a small group of parents whose children were participants in the Church's primary

---

[47] Israel Galindo, *The Craft of Christian Teaching: Essentials For Becoming a Very Good Teacher,* (Judson Press: Valley Forge, PA 1998), pg.19.

[48] Howard Gardner, *Frames of Mind, The Theory of Multiple Intelligences*, (New York: NY BasicBooks, 1983), pg.60-61.

and pre-teenage ministry at Harvest Christian Ministry. Instructors and staff, serving in the role of contextual associates, helped to guide this effort. This model of ministry was designed specifically for Harvest. The purpose of this particular model of ministry was to build upon, or establish at home, what was already shared during the Sunday morning learning experience. In this case, a select group of parents and guardians were trained using a biblically-based curriculum, which encouraged and empowered this group to share its acquired Christian knowledge within the framework of a home-setting.

One of the key elements of collecting data was to have participants observe the behaviors of their children while teaching the learning activities. They shared carefully crafted curriculum, which took into account the biblical and experiential knowledge of parents and guardians. Furthermore, this group became more equipped to share from within the framework of their daily lives. I believe children learn, in part, based on what they sense, see, and experience within the home. Therefore, it was my task to train and equip this group, in part, through training sessions and journal writing in which even the children could express their experiences. Parents and guardians were encouraged to augment individual lesson plans with the hope of expanding the learning experiences to which children were exposed. During the process, it was imperative to give parents and guardians spiritual clearance for innovation by allowing them to work within researcher-designed frameworks. This allowed for more creative interaction and ultimately led to a long-term relational model that could be shared with succeeding generations within the Harvest Congregation.

For two consecutive Sundays at my church, I recruited parents and guardians of children from ages three to twelve years to participate in a six-week biblically-based discipleship training session entitled *Project Harvest*. At the conclusion of the two-week recruitment effort, ten parents and guardians agreed to meet with me and subsequently fill out project registration forms. These forms gave participants an overview of *Project Harvest*, with the understanding that it was in conjunction with the requirements necessary for gathering results for my research project. They agreed to participate and commit themselves to six one-hour sessions, followed by an agreement to share in a ten-week home-based and biblically based child-oriented curriculum. This set the stage for the first *Project Harvest* session.

The second phase of the project consisted of ten individualized home-based lesson plans, which were administered by parents and guardians and shared with their children over a period of eight additional weeks. The goal of both phases of the project training was to equip parents and guardians with Christian discipleship principles so they, in turn, would be empowered to teach and model those principles to their children.

I found it necessary to assess the biblical knowledge level of the parents and guardians who took part in the church education project. The Holy Bible was the primary resource for learning, and it served as a guide throughout the educational process. I utilized both quantitative and qualitative research methods during the course of the learning experience. Participants were given pre and post-test evaluations in the process of assessing their needs and, subsequently, the needs of their children. At the conclusion of the project, participants, parents, guardians, and children orally shared their learning experiences during graduation exercises.

CHAPTER SEVEN

THE PROGRAM

Overview

I determined that a series of biblically based training sessions lasting six weeks would be beneficial to children and their parents and guardians.

- **Training session #1** helped participants understand their Christian faith by introducing them to the Holy Bible, its purpose, and how its passages would enhance the lives of them and their children.

- **Training session #2** helped parents and guardians use those scripture passages in order to articulate their own conversion experiences.

- **Training session #3** assisted parents in making connections between the Bible and the Christian ordinances of Holy Communion and Baptism.

- **Training session #4** assisted helped parents understandd participants in understanding the importance of their Christian testimony, changed life, and behavior, and how scripture passages would be useful for them and their children.

- **Training session #5** helped parents understand the role of prayer in their homes and how they will be able to model this discipline within their homes.

- **Training session #6** prepared participants to teach and model their Christian faith at home with their children through a series of ten individual lessons.

The second phase of the program gave parents and guardians the tools necessary to teach age-appropriate biblical lessons at home. Each training session included an instructional parent teaching guide in addition to a parent teaching log, which allowed them to assess their children level of understanding after each individual session.

- **Phase II Training session #1** parents and guardians to assist their children in learning about God's creation, and its meaning, documenting some of the things God created. There were also hands-on outdoor activities and individual age-appropriate coloring pages, puzzles, and word searches.

- **Training session #2** equipped parents to introduce to their children Scripture passages related to Jesus Christ, God's Son. Parents helped their children make connections between the importance of their birth and the birth of Jesus Christ. Parents also assisted their children in completing age-appropriate coloring pages, puzzles, and word search activities.

- **Training session #3** introduced students to Scripture passages related to God's word, the Holy Bible. Our team provided each parent and guardian with a flashlight in which they could assist their children in directing the light toward an open Bible. This activity helped to maximize the importance of using the Bible as a light and guide for living. Parents also shared in the singing of a song provided by our team that related to the Bible as God's Word. They sang together following the format of "The farmer and the dell."

- **Training session #4** centered on God's love. It directed parents toward Scripture passages that would help them to explain God's awesome love. In addition to the Scripture passages, parents assisted children in activities related to the Love of Jesus. Age-appropriate puzzles, coloring pages, and word searches were also included in this learning experience.

- **Training session #5** focused on God's miracles, and how they related to children. Parents shared Scripture passages and prepared a meal of fish and bread to further illustrate (as in Matthew 14:20) how Jesus Christ performed the miracle in the lives of those who followed him during his public ministry. Parents also assisted their children in completing age-appropriate puzzles, word searches, and coloring pages.

- **Training session #6** assisted parents and guardians in sharing with their children the importance of understanding their Christian beliefs. This was accomplished through assigned Scripture passages, which helped children make connections between their beliefs in the existence of objects in their midst and the belief of Jesus Christ as their Savior. This lesson concluded with a step-by-step prayer of confession and age-appropriate puzzles, word searches, and coloring pages.

- **Training session #7** gave parents the tools necessary to conduct prayer exercises with their children and family members. Parents identified Scripture passages related to prayer and then took part in a time of prayer with their children. Age-appropriate puzzles, word searches, and coloring pages accompanied the training session.

- **Training session #8** assisted parents in teaching their children the importance of obedience. Parents shared related Scripture passages to identify biblical characters who obeyed God. Age-appropriate puzzles, word searches, and coloring pages, were presented to the children by their parents to further develop this session.

- **Training session #9** assisted parents in explaining the definition of the Christian church, its purpose, and the role of its pastor as shepherd. Parents helped children make the connection between school and church as places; they also learned that the pastor, much like a shepherd, is the one who cares and nurtures the flock or congregation. Parents assisted their children in completing age-appropriate words searches, puzzles, and coloring pages.

• **Training session #10** directed parents toward Scripture passages which assisted them in explaining the purpose and the importance of Baptism and Holy Communion. In addition to Scripture passages, parents helped their children identify modern day symbols in helping to explain the importance of these church ordinances.

There were 15 children between the ages three and twelve years of age who took part in the project. The research was conducted through training sessions, in which parents and guardians using their Bible as their guide, were taught to understand their Christian faith, to teach and develop a Godly model, and to pray with their children. Preliminary indications suggest that when parents and guardians are equipped with this Christian discipleship knowledge, they will report that they have the necessary skills to help their school-aged children gain a clearer understanding of God's creation, His Son, His word, His love, His miracles, and their behaviors changed in the process. In addition to these guided lessons, this group of parents and guardians also reported that they helped their children gain a better understanding of prayer, their church, pastor, and the ordinances of Baptism and Holy Communion.

Ten parents and guardians agreed to participate in a series of training sessions and follow-up lessons in which they would teach their children at home. I was convinced that the knowledge and commitment of four contextual associates, who served in the roles of advisor and team members, were instrumental in carrying out this project.

They continued to work closely with parents and guardians in an attempt to help them navigate their school-aged children through many challenges. This group of contextual associates continues to teach children in a setting that is visual and participant-driven. There is now a greater degree of parental sup-port and response to prepared packets of learning materials that children are taking home and sharing with parents and guardians, thus continuing spiritual training beyond a one day a week experience.

CHAPTER EIGHT

THE PLAN

Training Session I

Session One
"Project Introduction/Overview"

The first session, project introduction/overview, followed the Sunday morning worship experience and was held in an adjoining room of the church. The goal of this session (APPENDIX A) was to assist participants in recognizing the importance of their call to teach and model their Christian faith in the home. I facilitated this session by reading Deuteronomy 6:4-9 and encouraged the participants to follow along.

> Hear, O Israel: The LORD our God, the LORD is one. Love the LORD your God with all your heart and with all your soul and with all your strength. These commandments that I give you today are to be upon your hearts. Impress them on your children. Talk about them when you sit at home and when you walk along the road, when you lie down and when you get up. Tie them as symbols on

your hands and bind them on your foreheads. Write them on the doorframes of your houses and on your gates.[49]

Two contextual associates were present to assist in setting up meeting space and helping to administer class materials (paper, pens, and the pre-test). At the beginning of the first session participants took a pre-test to gauge their level of participation in daily Bible reading, prayer, and the frequency with which they shared their faith with their children. I left the room while participants were tested and returned once they were finished. This initial session gave an overview of the six-week project and established the Bible as a guide for the project. Basic Bible facts were also shared. Each participant was given a post-it sticker and asked to write what they believed about God. Those post-its were then placed on a blackboard in full view of class. It helped to generate discussion. It was shared that the Bible was a collection of books, accepted by the Christian church as uniquely inspired by God, and thus authoritative in helping to provide guidelines for belief and behavior. I then helped to explain that the Bible is made up of the *Canon* or 66 books in the Old and New Testaments and is the inspired word of God. I had participants open their Bibles to 2 Timothy 3:16–17 and read the Scripture passage together.

> All Scripture is God-breathed and is useful for teaching, rebuking, correcting and training in righteousness, so that the man of God may be Thoroughly equipped for every good work[50]

---

[49] Deuteronomy 6:4-9 (New International Version).
[50] 2 Timothy 3:16-17 (New International Version).

Session Two
"Understanding My Christian Faith Part 1:

The second session focused on "Understanding My Christian Faith Part 1." I personally facilitated this session. The goals for this session were to: share the importance of spiritual education within their homes; to share how it would promote spiritual growth in their children now and well into their adult lives and and to identify and understand the God-given meaning of modeling Christian behavior. The word "faith" was posted on chart paper. Each participant was supplied with a post-it note in order to give their definition of faith. Participants posted their answers on the chart paper. I then shared the biblical definition of faith by referring to Hebrews 11:1–2, "Now faith is being sure of what we hope for and certain of what we do not see. This is what the ancients were commended for."[51]

Participants also read and were shown how to make reference to key Bible passages relating to faith in Jesus Christ. Furthermore, I reminded the participants that the theological background of Scripture related to their salvation, primarily how it is based on the Word of God. Romans 10:9–10 was shared with participants in helping them to understand that their salvation was based on the promises of God, the character of God, and

That if you confess with your mouth, "Jesus is Lord," and believe in your heart that God raised him from the dead, you will be saved. For it is with your heart that you believe and are justified, and it is with your mouth that you confess and are saved.[52]

Participants indicated that they understood the meaning of their faith and were given take-home assignments to complete, which consisted of documenting what they have learned about their role as biblical parents. I

---

[51] Hebrews 11:1-2 (New International Version).
[52] Romans 10:9-10 (New International Version).

believe that, at the conclusion of this session, parents and guardians were more equipped with the necessary knowledge to understand and share their Christian faith based on their classroom responses, post-test, and graduation speeches.

Session Three
"Understanding My Christian Faith, Part 2"

At the conclusion session three, parents and guardians were equipped with the necessary knowledge to understand their Christian faith and the church ordinances of Baptism and Holy Communion. I facilitated this session and focused on "Understanding My Christian Faith, Part 2." The word "ordinance" was posted on chart paper. Each participant was supplied with a post-it note and given the opportunity to give their definition. Once their answers were shared, this researcher explained the definition of Baptism and Holy Communion, using the following Bible passages, Matthew 3:13–17 and Matthew 26:26–28.

> Then Jesus came from Galilee to the Jordan to be baptized by John. But John tried to deter him, saying, "I need to be baptized by you, and do you come to me?" Jesus replied, "Let it be so now; it is proper for us to do this to fulfill all righteousness." Then John consented. As soon as Jesus was baptized, he went up out of the water. At that moment heaven was opened, and he saw the Spirit of God descending like a dove and lighting on him. And a voice from heaven said, "This is my Son, whom I love; with him I am well pleased."[53]

---

[53] Matthew 3:13-17 (New International Version).

While they were eating, Jesus took bread, gave thanks and broke it, and gave it to his disciples, saying, "Take and eat; this is my body." Then he took the cup, gave thanks and offered it to them, saying, "Drink from it, all of you. This is my blood of the covenant, which is poured out for many for the forgiveness of sins.[54]

The participants shared their own testimonies regarding their understanding of Baptism and Holy Communion. At least three indicated they had either been sprinkled or baptized at an early age and did not understand the significance in the life of the believer. They expressed their intent to be re-baptized following their sessions at Harvest Christian Ministries.

Session Four
"Developing a Godly Model for Children"

The primary goal of session four was to give participants the biblical tools necessary to teach and model their faith continually in their homes. From this session, participants gained a clearer understanding of their role as biblical parents: first, by becoming Godly examples of Christian discipleship, and secondly, by modeling their faith in their homes. It was suggested that one way they could model Christian behavior for the benefit of their child was to become cognizant of their own language and actions in the home.

This session covered topics such as the importance of sharing Christ with their children through Scripture, behavior and a changed life. This topic in particular was designed to emphasize the importance of being a consistent witness through personal experience. I read and discussed 2 Corinthians 5:17 and discussed 2 Corinthians 5:17, "Therefore, if anyone is in Christ, he is a new creation; the old has gone, the new has come."[55]

---

[54] Matthew 26:26-28 (New International Version).
[55] 2 Corinthians 5:17 (New International Version).

Participants were given a series of homework assignments, all of which focused on finding specific ways in which they could model Godly behavior during the course of the week. I discussed Christian modeling through testimony, that is, how parents and guardians lived out their faith on a daily basis. The example was shared of the Samaritan women in John 4:28, whose testimony impacted an entire community for Christ.

Session Five
"How to Pray Regularly with My children"

Session five focused primarily on having participants respond to the following: "Who taught you how to pray and at what age did you start praying?" I put emphasis on the importance of prayer and its relevance to the lives of the participants and their children based on Scripture. I also supplied participants with handouts to help guide them in how to pray as a family. I taught the acrostic ACTS, as a way of helping participants develop a varied prayer life.

A doration

C onfession

T hanksgiving

S supplication

The following Scripture passages were among those shared with participants to assist them in applying what they had learned about prayer by observing the model of Jesus Christ. In Mark 1:35, Jesus prays in private.

Very early in the morning, while it was still dark, Jesus got up, left the house and went off to a solitary place, where he prayed.[56]

---

[56] Mark 1:35 (New International Version).

In Luke 11:1, Jesus Christ modeled a life of prayer in the midst of his disciples prompting at least one of them to inquire. One day Jesus was praying in a certain place. When he finished, one of his disciples said to him, "Lord, teach us to pray, just as John taught his disciples"[57]

Session Six
"Conclusion, Preparing for Phase 2"

This final session with parents and guardians helped to prepare them to implement their ten-lesson home teaching curriculum. I reminded participants of the importance of recognizing the benefit of a church-based discipleship training course. In review, they were also given the opportunity to identify areas in which they had grown spiritually and how what they learned helped to strengthen them in their homes. The remainder of this session was set aside to help participants understand the purpose of the curriculum that had been implemented.

I distributed home training materials to each participant. This included a flashlight, camera, curriculum packet, coloring crayons, and heart stickers. Prior to distributing the materials, I reviewed the home lesson packet from start to finish and offered assistance to participants who had additional questions about the project. Participants acknowledged that they understood the instructions and expressed eagerness in beginning their home lessons.

Training Session II

During the next eight weeks parents and guardians shared assigned age-appropriate sessions with their school-aged children. The sessions (APPENDIX B) were scheduled in one-hour sessions and began with participants and their

---

[57] Luke 11:1 (New International Version).

children reading a Scripture passage, followed by activities designed to help children understand a particular biblical truth.

The first five sessions focused on God's creation, His Son, His word, His love, and His miracles. The session on God's creation required the family to take a walk in their community and discuss things God created such as trees, birds, the sun, and moon. The children were encouraged to photograph the things they witnessed and make a collage. Coloring pages and word puzzles related to the lessons were completed by the children, with assistance from parents and guardians.

The session on God's Son encouraged parents to discuss with their children the importance of personal gifts and how Jesus Christ is God's gift to the world. Parents discussed with their children where Christ was born and how He was sent as a gift for all of creation. They allowed the children to talk about the gifts they received at Christmas, and then helped them to make the connection between why they celebrate Christmas and how Jesus Christ is the gift for humanity. Parents asked their children to find their favorite gift and share why it was so important to them.

The session on God's Word was explained by having parents and guardians talk to their children about how God's Word should be a guide for living, sort of like a map or what is referred to as a global positioning system (GPS). Participants led children to a dark place in their homes or outside at night and opened their Bibles. Using a flashlight, children used the light source to highlight the words in the Bible. Children then used the light source to guide a few of their steps. A family song was shared about God's Word.

The session on God's love began with the children giving each member of the family a heart sticker and saying to them, "I love you." Then they had to explain why they loved that person. Parents discussed with children why it is important to love each other, especially family members. The group sang together the song, "Jesus Loves Me."

The session on God's miracles provided the necessary materials for parents and guardians to teach their children about God's miracles. At lunch or dinner, the family shared fish and bread. During their time together at the table, parents taught their children how Jesus took a little boy's lunch and multiplied it to feed five thousand people. They emphasized that Jesus took the meal, broke it, and blessed it. Parents prayed over the meal and shared their own stories of how Jesus worked a miracle through multiplying something in their life or the lives of their family.

The remaining five sessions were designed to help children understand their religious beliefs, prayer, their parents, church, pastor, Baptism and Holy Communion. The session on religious beliefs encouraged parents and guardians to have their children engage in age-appropriate family activities related to what they believed about themselves, God, and the world in which they live. One of the assignments had the children close their eyes and touch something familiar within their homes, such as a favorite toy or household object. Once their eyes were opened, they witnessed what they believed they had handled without actually first seeing the object.

The session on prayer required parents and guardians to assemble the family members and bow on their knees in a location within the home. They pressed their hands with each finger touching the other. They were asked to close their eyes and take turns saying a prayer. Parent or guardians were urged to share with their children an instance when God answered their prayers. The children were also asked to share their testimonies of answered prayer.

The session on the spiritual role of parents began and ended with discussions between parents and children. Parents or guardians assembled family members and explained cooking instructions related to a food item and why it was important to follow specific directions. The children were able to observe how their favorite meal was being prepared using explicit instructions.

The session on church and pastor made it possible for parents and guardians to define the roles and responsibilities of the church and pastor. The participants helped their children compare the surroundings at his or her school and those at the church. The school was defined as a place where children learn about subjects like reading, writing, and math; using separate handout, parents and guardians explained how the church is the place where people talk about God, Jesus and Love. There were handouts distributed to assist parents and guardians in making the connection between a shepherd, whose job it is to look after sheep with his rod and staff, and the job of a pastor to teach the people with the Bible.

The final parent-student session focused on two of the ordinances of the church, Baptism and Communion. For Baptism, parents and guardians assisted children identifying pictures of symbols in their community, such as a favorite place to eat, a traffic light or a familiar school sign. Participants explained what each symbol represented. In the same way, children learned that being baptized is symbol of a changed or new life in Christ. Baptism, according to *The Hiscox Standard Baptist Manual*, is the immersion of a person in water, on a profession of his faith in Christ, in, or into, the name of the Father, Son, and Holy Spirit.[58] The manual states further that the word baptism comes from the Greek baptize, which means "immerse" or "dip." Therefore, it cannot be applied properly to pouring or sprinkling.[59]

In order to discuss the ordinance of Communion, parents were urged to use a container of grape juice and a piece of bread, to try and make the connection between how the juice is a symbol for the blood Jesus shed for our sins on the cross. Likewise, the bread was to be used to help explain how Jesus' body was broken for us. Participants were required, in each assigned lesson, to keep parent-teaching logs for each child-centered home session. Those logs included the date, time, length of session, number of participants, observation, and follow up activities.

---

[58] Edward T. Hiscox, *The Hiscox Standard Baptist Manual* (Valley Forge, PA: Judson Press, 1985),
[59] Ibid, pg.81.

CHAPTER NINE

THE PROGRESS

*P*articipants reported they used a variety of methods when sharing and modeling Jesus Christ in the presence of their children. They were asked to rank the following indicators: their testimony, changed life, behavior, use of their Bibles, and providing insights from their Bibles. Participants could check as many methods as applied to this particular pre-test question. They reported an increase in the different methods they used to share Christ.

During graduation ceremonies at Harvest Christian Ministries, Ten participants shared some of their experiences in teaching and modeling Christian principles in their home. These were some of their experiences recorded on compact disc for use by the pastor and church congregation as it relates to the lessons parents and guardians learned during the process.

These are some of the responses recorded with permission, from participants:

Participant A:

> You really don't know God, until you try and teach God until you try and make it plain. Because your kids are going to go there and ask some questions, you really have to ask tough questions. My relationship with the Lord has strengthened. I'm just striving to

live by example to show our kids the way to go. This process was good for me personally because it really kind of forced me to look at the Word in a new way, You can't look at it through your own salvation, but for the salvation of your children. We just learned to be, I just learned to be really, really thankful.[60]

Participant B:

This process has really allowed us to ask our kids the question, "What would God say?" or even sitting them down in a tough situation and pulling out the Bible or praying more together when it's a difficult situation." As they move on, these tools will be those seeds that will be planted in them and when those situations happen in their lives and those tough times come and those good times, they will have the Lord to reflect on, to go to, to be their guiding post, what they stand on, their stronghold; that they won't be broken. I thank God for that.[61]

Participant C:

After doing some of the lessons, it's really taught me how to be more patient with my children because I realize that they are a reflection of me, they are going to do and act out the same things that I do, so if I don't change myself what's the purpose of even going through any of this stuff because they are not going to change either.[62]

---

[60] Participant A, "Project Harvest." [Oral Presentation, Harvest Christian Ministries, Baltimore, MD., May 26, 2009].

[61] Participant B "Project Harvest." [Oral Presentation, Harvest Christian Ministries, Baltimore, MD., May 26, 2009].

[62] Participant C, "Project Harvest." [Oral Presentation, Harvest Christian Ministries, Baltimore, MD., May 26, 2009].

Participants also expressed the moment they realized their home-based teaching interventions were making a difference in the lives of their school aged children.

Participant D:

> By the second week my son was coming to me and he was saying, "Mom, are we going to do some church study today? And I was like, wow, something is working here He's singing, he's asking questions, he's also interested in learning about God. So now, I realize that part of what we did was we were planting seeds. That's what project harvest is about to me, I felt like it was planting seeds and it also helped us grow spiritually as a family. Individually is important but also as a family.[63]

Another participant shared a similar testimony about her son.

Participant E:

> He was able to tell me every single day what we learned the next day what we learned the next week. He's still telling me what we learned and what he learned. He explained to me all about what the Bible means to him. He enjoyed the songs and he has taken every little bit and every little thing we did and basically joined them together and told you the correlation between This and that and God. And I really can say the lessons were actually informative for him and for me, because it helped me to also further enlighten my own spirit; and to see him actually learning everything that was taught just made me feel overwhelmed.[64]

---

[63] Participant D, "Project Harvest." [Oral Presentation, Harvest Christian Ministries, Baltimore, MD., May 26, 2009].

[64] Participant E," [Oral Presentation, Harvest Christian Ministries, Baltimore, MD., May 26, 2009].

Participant F:

> Before all of this, before our project, when he would hear the gospel music or he would see the Bible, he always related it to mom. He would say Oh, that's grandma. But now I am happy to say when I turn on spirituals or we are reading the Bible he's relating it to me; he would say me. He would say, "mommy is that Jesus? You are playing Jesus." That's God, and I'm happy about that because I've gone through my own transition.[65]

Participants say they were assured that their prescribed interventions will have lasting effects in the lives of their children.

Participant G:

> My whole thing is that I hope that we will continue to grow together and that when he is older he will teach that to his children.[66]

Participant H:

> The biggest thing that I took away from it was letting go or control. I'm a little bit of a control freak and I like to be in charge and every-thing is planned A, B, C D. Giving up that control was my freedom. I'm a worry free parent now because you have the Bible. That's exactly how I feel. I have a tool. I have a resource I can go to no matter what the situation, how bad how good, how complex.[67]

The children also provided evidence they were gaining knowledge from the intervention project. These comments were shared by a seven and ten year old.

---

[65] Participant F, "Project Harvest." [Oral Presentation, Harvest Christian Ministries, Baltimore, MD., May 26, 2009].

[66] Participant G "Project Harvest." [Oral Presentation, Harvest Christian Ministries, Baltimore, MD., May 26, 2009].

[67] Participant H, "Project Harvest." [Oral Presentation, Harvest Christian Ministries, Baltimore, MD., May 26, 2009].

Child Participant I:

> It was a fun activity and it felt like I was learning more and having fun and I was doing it with my mother, my brother and my sister. We started drawing and coloring and then we started reading the Bible and it got to be really fun. And I learn that the Lord can help us.[68]

Child Participant J:

> I learned to obey my parents, grandparents and family because the Lord speaks through people to speak to us. I'm very happy I learned this. The Bible gives me good answers. The Bible leads me into the right direction. It also has definitions in the back in case I'm struggling. During the project I learned there were 66 books in the Bible, 27 books in the New Testament and 39 in the Old Testament.[69]

---

[68] Child Participant I, "Project Harvest." [Oral Presentation, Harvest Christian Ministries, Baltimore, MD., May 26, 2009].

[69] Child Participant J," Project Harvest." [Oral Presentation, Harvest Christian Ministries, Baltimore, MD., May 26, 2009].

CHAPTER TEN

THE PARTING WORDS

SUMMARY, REFLECTIONS, AND CONCLUSIONS

*T*his project attempted and was successful in reaching children ages three through twelve years whom I believed would benefit from biblical instruction from their parent or guardian at home. Therefore, it was my intent to reach out to the adults in my congregation and equip them with the necessary biblical tools to teach and model Christian discipleship principles. As a result of six weeks of intensive biblical training in which I provided, parents and guardians responded to the degree which responded to the degree to which they realized the importance of the assignment. In addition, the same participants reached a level of comfort in which they could share their Christian faith with their children, other family members and friends. Throughout this process, parents were eager to learn and were eager to ask questions that would strengthen their own faith.

It was with this renewed enthusiasm and knowledge that parents and guardians were able to apply what they had learned with their children. During a period of eight weeks, participants, equipped with individualized and age-appropriate lesson plans, taught their children the basics of the Christian Faith. This was accomplished using lesson material that piqued the interest of children within their home. I am convinced now as I was then that the successes accomplished within my context helped to motivate parents and guardians within my congregation, but also laid a foundation in which participants could continue to teach and model their Faith.

I continue to witness the spiritual fruit of this project each and every Sunday when I interact with participants--a number of them who have begun their college careers. As I reflect further, I am certain this project can be replicated within other contexts, and I am mindful that such a program must be designed to help complement the increasingly mobile lifestyle of parents and guardians.

This project was birthed out of my own upbringing in which the faith was taught and modeled within my home. In addition, I was privileged to share insights from this project with my own three adult children and two grandchildren. I believe that, in so many ways, their commitment to the Lord Jesus Christ presently is because of the attempt of my wife and I to become intentional about teaching and modeling biblical principles within our own home. I can truly say I am possessed with a re-birth of hope within my heart, soul, mind and spirit and am able to testify that my personal faith has grown through the process. I continue to embrace the words of the Apostle Paul in his letter to the church in Philippi (Philippians1:3–6).

> I thank my God every time I remember you. In all my prayers for all of you, I always pray with joy because of your partnership in the gospel from the first day until now, being confident of this, that he who began a good work in you will carry it on to completion until the day of Christ Jesus.[70]

---

[70] Philippians 1:3–6 (New International Version).

APPENDIX A

PARTICIPANT TRAINING
SESSION ONE

Phase I (Parents and Guardians only)

Session 1	Session 2	Session 3	Session 4	Session 5	Session 6
Project Introduction /Overview	Understanding My Christian Faith (Pt. 1).	Understanding My Christian Faith (Pt.2)	Developing a Godly model	How to pray with My children	Session Conclusion/ Preparing for Phase 2
Time Allotted: 1 hour	Time Allotted: 1 hour	Time Allotted: 1 hour	Time Allotted: 1 hour	Time Allotted: 1 hour	Time Allotted: 1 hour
Facilitator	Facilitator	Facilitator	Facilitator	Facilitator	Facilitator
The primary goal of this session is to give parents and guardians an overview of the six week, course, its expectations and content. This setting will also establish the Bible as guide for the project.	At the conclusion of this session, parents and guardians will be equipped with the necessary knowledge to understand their Christian Faith.	At the conclusion of this session, parents and guardians will be equipped to share their Christian faith and the church ordinances of Baptism and Communion.	At the conclusion of this session, parents and guardians will be equipped to teach and model Christian behavior in the presence of their children in the home.	At the conclusion of this session, parents and guardians will be equipped with the necessary knowledge in order to participate in family prayer and to model a prayer filled life.	The primary goal of this session is to conclude the course phase I of the course and prepare participants for phase 2, in which they will share what they have learned with their children at home.

HARVEST CHRISTIAN MINISTRIES SESSION PLAN

Instructor:	Date:
Course Title: Introduction/Overview	**Session Number 1**
Unit: Christian Discipleship	

Parental Performance Goals:
- Recognize the importance of their role as teachers and models in the home.
- Understand the purpose of the curriculum that will be taught and implemented.
- Articulate their spiritual background in survey format.

Instructional Objective:
The primary goal of this session is to give parents and guardians an overview of the six-week course, its expectations and content. This setting will also establish the Bible as a guide for the project.

Rationale: It is necessary for parents and guardians to learn Christian discipleship principles in order to model Christ in the presence of their children.

Instructional Procedures:
  Focusing Event: Session will begin with a group prayer, with each person sharing their understanding and expectations for the course.

  Teaching Procedure: Direct teaching which will allow the instructor to provide information within a structure that enables participants to attain the objectives at a master level. Sessions will be biblically based and interactive, thus giving participants ample opportunity to ask questions and to model home teaching plans.

Procedures:
1. Explain the importance of the curriculum and how participants will benefit.
2. Give overview of six week course
3. Administer course pre-test
  Formative Check: "From this session, I have learned why it is important to enroll in a biblical based training course within my church. This course will give me a biblical foundation to teach Christian discipleship principles within my home."

  Student Participation: Participants will receive course syllabus and take pre-test.

  Closure: Close with a group prayer.

  Materials needed: Holy Bible, handouts

The BIBLE as a BILICAL GUIDE

The Bible is a collection of books, accepted by the Christian church as uniquely inspired by God, and thus authoritative, providing guidelines for belief and behavior. The Bible is made up of the *Canon* or 66 books in the Old and New Testaments and is the inspired word of God. Discuss **2 Timothy 3:16–17**. [16]All Scripture is God-breathed and is useful for teaching, rebuking, correcting and training in righteousness, [17]so that the man of God may be thoroughly equipped for every good work.

Genesis	Ezra	Joel
Exodus	Nehemiah	Amos
Leviticus	Esther	Obadiah
Numbers	Job	Jonah
Deuteronomy	Psalm	Micah
Joshua	Proverbs	Nahum
Judges	Ecclesiastes	Habakkuk
Ruth	Song of Solomon	Zephaniah
1 Samuel	Isaiah	Haggai
2 Samuel	Jeremiah	Zechariah
1 Kings `	Lamentations	Malachi
2 Kings	Ezekiel	Matthew
1 Chronicles	Daniel	Mark
2 Chronicles	Hosea	Luke

John	1 Timothy	1 John
Acts	2 Timothy	2 John
Romans	Titus	3 John
1 Corinthians	Philemon	Jude
2 Corinthians	Hebrews	Revelation
Galatians	James	
Ephesians	1 Peter	
Philippians	2 Peter	
Colossians		
1 Thessalonians		
2 Thessalonians		

BIBLE FACTS

The Old Testament has...
- 39 books
- 929 chapters
- 23,214 verses
- 593,493 words
- Longest book: Jeremiah
- Shortest book: Obadiah

The New Testament has...
- 27 books
- 260 chapters
- 7,959 verses
- 181,253 words
- Longest book: Acts
- Shortest book in the Bible: 3 John (least number of words, 2 John has more words, but one fewer verses.)
- 5 history books (Acts and the Gospels: Matthew, Mark, Luke, John)
- 21 letters (epistles)
- 1 book of prophecy (Revelation)

1. Books of Moses and the Law	2. History books	3. Wisdom books	4. Prophets' books	5. Gospels
The Pentateuch: Genesis Exodus Leviticus Numbers Deuteronomy	About God's chosen people, Israel Joshua Judges Ruth 1 Samuel 2 Samuel 1 Kings 2 Kings 1 Chronicles 2 Chronicles Ezra Nehemiah Esther	Job Psalms Proverbs Ecclesiastes Song of Solomon	Beginning with the most major five first Isaiah Jeremiah Lamentations Ezekiel Daniel Hosea Joel Amos Obadiah Jonah Micah Nahum Habakkuk Zephaniah Haggai Zechariah Malachi	Jesus' life and the way of salvation Matthew Mark Luke John

6. History of the early church	7. Paul's letters	8. Other letters	9. Apocalypse
Acts of the Apostles	Romans 1 Corinthians 2 Corinthians Galatians Ephesians Philippians Colossians 1 Thessalonians 2 Thessalonians 1 Timothy 2 Timothy Titus Philemon Hebrews	James 1 Peter 2 Peter 1 John 2 John 3 John Jude	Revelation

HARVEST CHRISTIAN MINISTRIES SESSION PLAN

Instructor:
Course Title: Understanding my Christian Faith/Session Number 2
Unit: Christian Discipleship
Parental Performance Goals: • Recognize the importance of spiritual education within their home and how it will promote spiritual growth in their children and in their own lives. • Identify and understand the God-given meaning of modeling Christian behavior.
Instructional Objective: At the conclusion of this session, parents and guardians will be equipped with the necessary knowledge to understand their Christian Faith.
Rationale: It is necessary for parents and guardians to learn Christian discipleship principles in order to model Christ in the presence of their children.
Session Content: a. Understanding your Christian faith b. Instructing children in their faith

Instructional Procedures:
    Focusing Event: Session will begin with a group prayer with each person praying for their families.
 	
    Teaching Procedure: Direct teaching which will allow the instructor to provide information within a structure that enables participants to attain the objectives at a level of mastery. Session will be biblically-based and interactive, thus giving participants ample opportunity to ask questions and to model home teaching plans.
 	
• The word "faith" will be posted on chart paper. Participants will be supplied with a post-it note and give their definition of faith. Participants will post their answer on the chart paper.
• Instructor will then give the definition of faith which will be referred to for the remaining sessions.
• Participants will read and reference key Bible passages relating to faith in Jesus Christ.
• Instructor will give theological background of scripture, Hebrews 11:1-2.
• Participants and instructors will define the term "salvation." Instructor will guide participants through Understanding My Christian Faith handout #1 with the use of a Bible.
• Instructor and participants will summarize lesson on faith by completing handout #2.
 	
Formative Check: Handout #3
    Intended response: From this session I've learned that my role as a biblical parent is to first understand my Christian faith. One way one I can gain a better understanding of my Christian faith is through Holy Scripture. I then share that understanding with my children.

Student Participation: Participants will read relevant Scripture passages which address salvation. They will become familiar with where to find passages.

Closure: Summarize the session materials and close with a group prayer.

Materials And Aid: Holy Bible, age appropriate handouts, laptop computer, projector, screen

Session Two
Understanding My Christian Faith

1. **Your salvation is based on the Word of God**. The Bible states in John 3:16 that God wants you to know that you have eternal life. Read the verse and underline it in your Bible.

2. **Your salvation is based on the Promises of God**. What are the promises found in the following verse?

   "That if you_____with your mouth, "Jesus is Lord, "and _____in your heart that God raised him from the dead, _____
   (Romans 10:9).

3. **Your salvation is based on the Character of God**. A promise is only as reliable the person who makes it. That is why the assurance of your salvation rests on God's Character.
   What do these verses teach about His character?
   God, who has called you into fellowship with his Son Jesus Christ our Lord, is _____" (1 Corinthians 1:9). "The one who calls you is _____and he will do it" (1 Thessalonians 5:24)

4. **Your salvation is based on the Spirit of God**. Read Ephesians 1:13–14. What is the seal given by God as a guarantee of His promise?

   _____

Understanding My Christian Faith
Session Two: My Faith

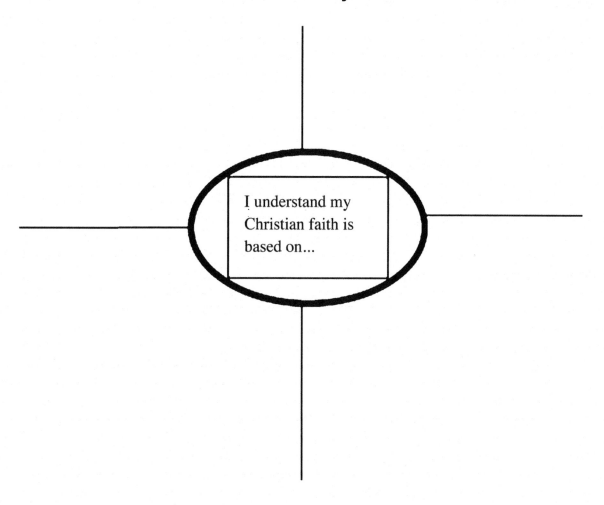

Understanding My Christian Faith
Session 2: My Faith

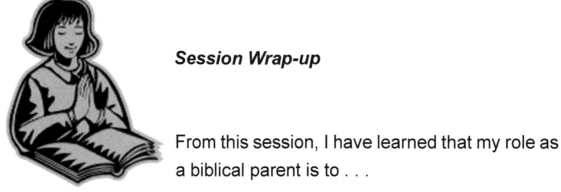

Session Wrap-up

From this session, I have learned that my role as a biblical parent is to . . .

_____

_____

_____

_____

_____

_____

_____

One way I can understand my faith this week is to . . .

_____

_____

_____

_____

_____

_____

_____

HARVEST CHRISTIAN MINISTRIES SESSION PLAN

Instructor:	Date:
Course Title: Understanding My Christian Faith Part 2	**Session Number 3**
Unit: Christian Discipleship	

Parental Performance Goals:
- Recognize the importance of spiritual education within their home and how it will promote spiritual growth in their children and in their own lives.
- Identify and understand the God-given intent of modeling Christian behavior

Instructional Objective: At the conclusion of this session, parents and guardians will be equipped with the necessary knowledge to understand their Christian faith and the church ordinances of Baptism and Communion.

Rationale: It is necessary for parents and guardians to learn Christian discipleship principles in order to model Christ in the presence of their children.

Session Content:
    a. Understanding the ordinance of Baptism
    b. Understanding the ordinance of Holy Communion

Instructional Procedures:
    Focusing Event: Session will begin with a group prayer with each person praying for their families.

    Teaching Procedure: Direct teaching which will allow the instructor to provide information within a structure that enables participants to attain the objectives at a level of mastery. Session will be biblically-based and interactive, thus giving participants ample opportunity to ask questions and to model home teaching plans.

- The word "ordinance" will be posted on chart paper. Participants will be supplied with a post-it note and give their definition of ordinance. Participants will post their answer on the chart paper.
- Instructor will then give the definition of ordinance and refer participants to the following Scripture passages. Matthew 3:13–17, Matthew 26:26–28.
- Participants will read and reference key Bible passages relating to faith in Jesus Christ.
- Instructor will give theological background of shared Scripture.
- Participants and instructors will define the term "Baptism" and "Holy Communion." Instructor will guide participants through Understanding My Christian Faith handout #1 with the use of a Bible.
- Instructor and participants will summarize lesson on Church ordinances by completing handout #2.

Formative Check: Handout #3

> **Intended response:** From this session I've learned that my role as a biblical parent is to first understand my Christian faith. One way one I can gain a better understanding of my Christian faith is through Holy Scripture. I then share that understanding with my children.
>
> **Student Participation:** Participants will read relevant passages which address salvation. They will become familiar on where to find key passages.
>
> **Closure:** Summarize the session materials and close with a group prayer.
>
> **Materials And Aid:** Holy Bible, age-appropriate handouts

Session 3

Understanding My Christian Faith
Part 2

1. Jesus commanded baptism in **Matthew 28:19–20**. He said, "¹⁹Therefore go and make disciples of all nations, _____ in the name of the Father, of the Son and of the Holy Spirit, ²⁰and _____ I have commanded you. And surely I am with you always, to the very end of the age."

2. Jesus set the example by being baptized in **Matthew 3:13–14**. ¹³Then Jesus came from Galilee to the Jordan_____. ¹⁴But John tried to deter him, saying, "I need to be baptized by you, and do you come to me?"

3. The New Testament Church, to which Harvest Christian Ministries adheres, requires new believers to be baptized through total "immersion" of a person in water, as a profession of faith in Jesus Christ.

4. Christians celebrate the sacrament of Holy Communion as a way of "giving thanks" for the love of God poured out in the life, death, and resurrection of Jesus.

5. In **Matthew 26:26–28** gives a biblical account of Holy Communion. ²⁶While they were eating, Jesus took bread, gave thanks and broke it, and gave it to his disciples, saying,"_____"

6. That same passage records, ²⁷Then he (Jesus) took the cup, gave thanks and offered it to them, saying, "Drink from it, all of you. ²⁸_____, _____which is poured out for many for the forgiveness of sins.

Understanding My Christian Faith
Session 3: My Faith

Session Wrap-up

From this session, I have learned that Baptism is an ordinance of the Church . . .

_____

_____

_____

_____

_____

_____

_____

One way I can model the holy ordinance of Baptism is to . . .

_____

_____

_____

_____

_____

_____

Understanding My Christian Faith
Session 3: Holy Communion

Session Wrap-up

From this session, I have learned that Holy Communion is an ordinance of the Church . . .

_____

_____

_____

_____

_____

_____

One way I can model the ordinance of Holy Communion is to . . .

_____

_____

_____

_____

_____

HARVEST CHRISTIAN MINISTRIES SESSION PLAN

Instructor:	Date:
Course Title: Developing a Godly Model for Children	**Session Number** 4
Unit: Christian Discipleship	

Parental Performance Goals: • Recognize the importance of spiritual education within their home and how it will promote spiritual growth in their children their own lives. • Identify and understand the God-given meaning of modeling Christian behavior.
Instructional Objective: At the conclusion of this session, parents and guardians will be equipped with the necessary knowledge to serve as a model for their children.
Rationale: It is necessary for parents and guardians to learn Christian discipleship principles in order to serve as a model Christ in the presence of their children.

Lesson Content:
   a. Review Faith and Salvation is based on: Word of God, Promises of God, Character of God, and Spirit of God.
   b. Modeling Christian Behavior

Instructional Procedures:

Focusing Event: Session will begin with a group prayer, with each person praying for their families.

Teaching Procedure: Direct teaching which will allow the instructor to provide information within a structure that enables participants to attain the objectives at a level of mastery. Session will be biblically-based and interactive, thus giving participants ample opportunity to ask questions and to model home teaching plans.

1. (Warm up activity) "My role as a parent" will be on chart paper. Participants will receive 3 Post-its and write their response and place them on the chart paper. Instructor and participants will review responses.
2. Instructor will guide participants through Scripture passages related to their biblical role as parents. Deuteronomy 6:7–9.
3. Participants will model behavior by using the Bible and handout #2 (Modeling my Christian Faith) with instructor.
4. Instructor and participants will summarize lesson on modeling faith by completing graphic organizer on modeling Christ.

Formative Check: "From this session, I've learned that my role as a biblical parent is to first become a Godly example of Christian discipleship. One way I can model Christian behavior for the benefit of my child is to become cognizant of what I say and do."

a. **Student Participation:** A series of classroom role play procedures, as they relate to teaching their children biblical principles.
b. **Closure:** Summarize the session materials and close with a group prayer.

Materials And Aid: Holy Bible, age appropriate handouts, laptop computer, projector, screen

Session 4
Developing a Godly Model

1. I can share Christ through my **TESTIMONY.** In John 4:28 ᵃ Samaritan woman met Christ and responded by leaving her water jar, the woman went back to the town and said to the people, —————————— ——————". Could this is the Christ?" They came out of the town and made their way toward him.

2. I can share Christ though a **CHANGED LIFE**. The apostle Paul states in 2 Corinthians 5:17 what he learned from personal experience. Therefore, if anyone is in Christ,_____; the old has gone, the new has come!

3. I can share Christ though my **BEHAVIOR.** The Bible suggests in Galatians 5:16 that if I_____I will not gratify the desires of_____ .

4. I can share Christ with my **BIBLE.** In 2 Timothy 3:16–17, the Bible suggests that all Scripture is _____ and is useful for teaching, rebuking, correcting and training in righteousness, so that the man of God may be _____

_____

Developing a Godly model
Session 4: My role

Session Wrap-up

From this session, I have learned that my role as a biblical parent is to . . .

_____
_____
_____
_____
_____
_____

One way I can model Godly behavior this week is . . .

_____
_____
_____
_____
_____
_____

HARVEST CHRISTIAN MINISTRIES SESSION PLAN

Instructor:	Date:
Course Title: How pray regularly with my children	**Session Number 5**
Unit: Christian Discipleship	

Parental Performance Goals:
- Recognize the importance of prayer practiced within their home and how it will promote spiritual growth in their children their own lives.
- Demonstrate how to pray with their children

Instructional Objective: At the conclusion of this session, parents and guardians will be equipped with the necessary knowledge in order to participate in family prayer and to model a prayer-filled life.

Rationale: It is necessary for parents and guardians to learn Christian discipleship principles in order to model Christ in the presence of their children.

Lesson Content:
   a. Review modeling Godly behavior
   b. How to pray regularly with your children

Instructional Procedures:

    Focusing Event: Session will begin with a group prayer, with each person praying for their families.

    Teaching Procedure: Direct teaching which will allow the instructor to provide information within a structure that enables participants to attain the stated objectives at a level of mastery. Session will be biblically-based and interactive, thus giving participants ample opportunity to ask questions and to model home teaching plans.

1. Have participants respond to the following:
   - Who taught you how to pray?
   - At what age did you start praying?
2. Instructor will share the importance of prayer and its relevance in their children's lives through the Scripture passage Mark 1:35
3. Instructor will guide participants with the Bible through handout #1 which will assist them in how to pray as a family.
4. Instructor will use model how to pray using the ACTS acronym.
5. Participants will use acrostics ACTS to write a four sentence prayer. Each person will be asked to share his or her prayer with the group.

    Formative Check: "From this session, I have a learned why it is important to pray regularly with my children. One way I can model teaching my children to pray is to pray in their presence."

    Student Participation: A series of classroom role play procedures, as they relate to praying with children.

    Closure: Close with a group prayer.

    Materials And Aid: Holy Bible, age appropriate handouts, laptop computer, projector, screen

Session Five

How to Pray as a Family

1. Jesus set the example for us (read **Mark 1:35**)
What does this passage say about Jesus' prayer life?

_____

2. Jesus taught the necessity of prayer (read **Luke 18:1**)

_____

3. What did the disciples ask Jesus to teach them (read **Luke 11:1**)?

_____

4. Why should we pray continually (read 1 **Thessalonians 5:17**)?

_____

The acrostic ACTS will assist you to begin developing your prayer life.

A doration
C onfession
T hanksgiving
S upplication

How to Pray

Use the acrostic ACTS to develop a prayer.

- *Adoration* is praise focusing on who God is.
- *Confession* is acknowledging your sins before God.
- *Thanksgiving* is expressing gratitude to God for specific acts.
- *Supplication* is making requests and expressing desires to God.

A: _____

C: _____

T: _____

S: _____

How to Pray Regularly with Your Children

Session Five: Family Prayer

Session Wrap-up

From this session, I have learned why it is important to pray regularly with my children based upon the following Scripture passages . . .

_____

_____

_____

_____

_____

_____

_____

One way I can prioritize prayer with my child is to . . .

_____

_____

_____

_____

_____

_____

HARVEST CHRISTIAN MINISTRIES SESSION PLAN

Instructor:	Date:
Course Title: Conclusion/Preparing for Phase two	**Session Number 6**
Unit: Christian Discipleship	

Parental Performance Goals:
- Recognize the importance and benefit of a church-based discipleship training course.
- Identify areas in which participants have grown spiritually and how those strengths will now be modeled in the home.
- Understand the purpose of the curriculum that will be implemented.

Instructional Objective: The primary goal of this session is to conclude the course (Phase one) and prepare participants for phase two, in which they will share what they have learned with their children at home.

Rationale: It is necessary for parents and guardians to learn Christian discipleship principles in order to model Christ in the presence of their children.

Lesson Content:
a. Phase one course conclusion and introduction of Phase two.
b. Receive answers to any questions regarding course format and Phase two implementation.

Instructional Procedures:

Focusing Event: Session will begin with a group prayer, with each person praying for their families.

Teaching Procedure: Direct teaching which will allow the instructor to provide information within a structure that enables participants to attain the objectives at a level of mastery. Session will be biblically-based and interactive, thus giving participants ample opportunity to ask questions and to model home teaching plans.
1. Participants will share their desire and their willingness to share home discipleship sessions.
2. Give overview of lessons for Phase 2.

Formative Check: "From this session, I have a learned why it is important to avail myself to a biblical-based training course within my church. This session will give me a biblical foundation to teach Christian discipleship principles within my home."

Student Participation: A series of classroom role play procedures, as they relate to sharing discipleship principles with their children.

Closure: Close with a group prayer.

Materials And Aid: Holy Bible, age appropriate handouts.

APPENDIX B
CHILDREN'S TRAINING TWO

PROJECT PHASE TWO TIMELINE

Time Line

Phase II (Children)

GOD'S CREATION	GOD'S SON	GOD'S WORD	GOD'S LOVE	GOD'S MIRACLES
Scripture: Genesis 1:1 Genesis 1:27 Facilitator: Parent/Guardian Allotted time: 1 hour	Scripture: John 3:16 Facilitator: Parent/Guardian Allotted time: 1 hour	Scripture: Psalms 119:105 Facilitator: Parent/Guardian Allotted time: 1 hour	Scripture: Romans 5:8 Facilitator: Parent/Guardian Allotted time: 1 hour	Scripture: Matthew 14:19–20 Facilitator: Parent/Guardian Allotted time: 1 hour
Activity: Take family walk and discuss trees, birds, moon, sun (bugs/creature). Take photographs of God's creation. Allow children to make a collage.	Activity: Talk about gifts they've received or given.	Activity: Use flashlight or candle to demonstrate how light dispels darkness. Allow the light to reflect on an open Bible.	Activity: Sing printed version of "Jesus Loves Me. "Give each family member love stickers. Share your love for them, even recalling their birth.	Activity: Include fish and bread as part of a dinner menu.
Materials: 1.Color page of world 2.Creation Puzzle	Materials: 1. Color page of Jesus in manger. 2. Christ word search.	Materials: 1.Candle or flashlight 2.Color candle page	Materials: 1.Heart stickers, 2. Color heart. Puzzle.	Materials: 1. Color page of boy's lunch with Jesus. 2.Miracle puzzle.

HARVEST CHRISTIAN MINISTRIES

SESSION PLAN

PHASE 2

Instructor: Parent/Guardian	**Date:**
Course Title: God's Creation	**Session Number 1**
Unit: Christian Discipleship	

Instructional Objective:
By the end of this session, your child will have a clearer understanding of who God has made each of them to become. Lessons are designed for ages (3-5), (6-9), (10-12).

Rationale: If children are able to make the connection between an all-knowing and all-powerful God, then they will place a greater value on their individual lives.

Session Content:
   a. Age-appropriate biblically-based sessions outlined in training packet.
   b. Parents and guardians will incorporate sessions which will address their child's spiritual, emotional, cognitive, and physical needs.

Instructional Procedures:
   1. Parent or guardian will open Bible to Genesis 1:1 and 1:27 and together read passages aloud with child.
   2. Parent or guardian will identify a path within their neighborhood and walk together to chosen location and then return home.
   3. Parent or guardian will point out the things God made and have child take photographs of each creation. Parent will assist child in coloring age appropriate pictures and completing a word search or puzzle.

   Closure: Review pictures taken and close with a group prayer.

Materials needed: Holy Bible, handouts, camera, coloring crayons

PARENT TEACHING GUIDE

SESSION TOPIC

GOD'S CREATION

STEP 1: • **Set a time for lesson** 	STEP 2: • **Pick a place**
STEP 3: • **Have supplies on hand. Holy Bible, handouts, camera, coloring crayons** 	STEP 4: • **Open Bible to Genesis 1:1 and Genesis 1:27 and read verses**
STEP 5: • **Share definition of create.** **BEGIN ACTIVITY** 1. **Locate a place in which you and your children can walk. Point out things God has created.** 2. **Assist children in taking pictures of what they see.**	CREATE • **"To make something new"** **END ACTIVITY** 1. **Assist children in drawing pictures and completing word puzzles.** 2. **Develop or print pictures and paste them on collage.**

PARENT TEACHING GUIDE

Daily Log

Date:	Time:
Length of session:	Number of children participants:
Personal Observations: Signature: _____	Is follow-up needed?

Creation

Scripture highlight:

"In the beginning God created the heavens and the earth."
Genesis 1:1.

Then God said, "Let us make man in our image, in our likeness, and let them rule over the fish of the sea and the birds of the air, over the livestock, over all the earth, [a] and over all the creatures that move along the ground." 27 So God created man in his own image, in the image of God he created him; male and female he created them.
Genesis 1:26–27.

What does it mean to create? (All Ages)

Create means to "make something new." Genesis tells us that God is the creator of all things. You can find many things God created in Genesis Chapter 1.

Things God created? (All Ages)

1. Light
2. The sky
3. The seas
4. Plants
5. Living creatures
6. People

Family Activity: (All Ages)

- Choose an activity that focuses on God's creation. Take a walk in your community and look for things that God created. Remind children that it is God's creation you're enjoying together.

- Take the family camera and have children to capture what they observe during the walk. Once returning home, have them to use pictures to create a collage, using the images which impacted them the most.

Ages (6-9) (10-12)

In His Image

Collage

Ages (3-5) (6-9)

In the beginning God created the heaven and the earth (Genesis 1:1)

Ages (10-12)

And It Was Very Good

In the beginning God created the heavens and the earth. Genesis 1:1 (NIV)

This puzzle is based on Genesis 1:1-2:4a (NIV)

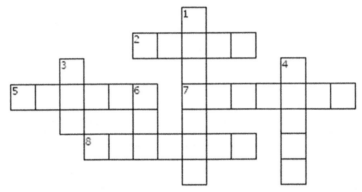

ACROSS

2. Creatures with feathers and wings, usually able to fly

5. Living things that have a stem, leaves, roots, and sometimes flowers

7. Living things that can move and eat

8. The space that seems to be over the earth like a dome

DOWN

1. To cause something to exist, or to make

3. General term for the human race, or any member or group of it

4. The planet on which we live

6. The waters that cover most of the surface of the earth

CREATED	BIRDS	ANIMALS	EARTH
HEAVENS	PLANTS	MAN	SEA

www.sermon4kids.com

HARVEST CHRISTIAN MINISTRIES

SESSION PLAN

PHASE 2

Instructor: Parent/Guardian	**Date:**
Course Title: God's Son	**Session Number 2**
Unit: Christian Discipleship	

Instructional Objective:
By the end of this session, your child will have a clearer understanding of why God sent his Son Jesus into the world. Sessions are designed for ages (3-5), (6-9), (10-12).

Rationale: If children are able to make the connection between an all-knowing and all-powerful God, then they will place a greater value on their individual lives.

Session Content:
  a. Age-appropriate biblically-based sessions outlined in training packet.
  b. Parents and guardians will incorporate sessions which will address their child's spiritual, emotional, cognitive, and physical needs.

Instructional Procedures:
  1. Parent or guardian will open a Bible to John 3:16 and Matthew 2:1–2 and together read passages aloud with child.
  2. Parent or guardian will have child to identify a special gift and place it at one central location.
  3. Parent or guardian will assist child with finding the birthplace of Jesus and themselves on the maps provided. They will then assist child in coloring age-appropriate pictures and completing a word search or puzzle.

  Closure: Close with a group prayer.

  Materials needed: Holy Bible, handouts, personal gifts

PARENT TEACHING GUIDE

SESSION TOPIC

GOD'S SON

STEP 1: • Set a time for lesson	**STEP 2:** • Pick a place
STEP 3: • Open packet to God's Son.	**STEP 4:** • Open Bible to John 3:16 and Matthew 2:1-2 and read passages aloud.
STEP 5: • Parent or Guardian will have child identify their special gift and place it at one central location. • Assist child in finding birthplace of Jesus and themselves on the maps provided.	**STEP 5:** • Assist child in coloring age-appropiate pictures and word search puzzle. • Close session with prayer.

PARENT TEACHING GUIDE

Daily Log

Date:	Time:
Length of session:	Number of children participants:
Personal Observations Signature: _____	Is follow-up needed?

Jesus Christ

Scripture highlight:

"For God so loved the world that he gave his one and only Son, that whoever believes in him shall not perish but have eternal life. *John 3:16.*

Who is Jesus?

Name given to the heavenly Son of God and the earthly son of Joseph and Mary. He was sent to save God's people from their sins and can still save us today.

Where was Jesus born?

_____

Where were you born?

_____

Family Activity (All Ages)

Talk to your children about where Christ was born and how he was sent as a gift for all of us. Allow the children to talk about the gifts they received at Christmas, and then make the connection between why we celebrate Christmas. Ask your children to find their favorite gift and explain why it is some important to them.

Ages (6-9)

Where was Jesus born?

_____

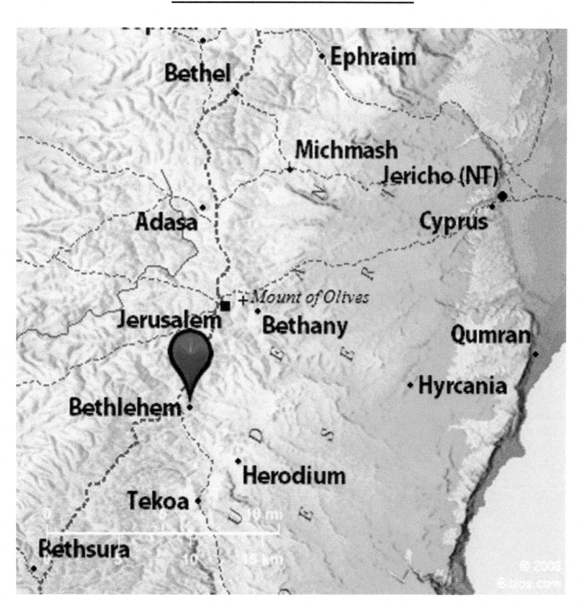

www.biblos.com

Where were you born?

_____

Ages (3-5) (6-9)

www.sermon4kids.com

Ages (10-12)
The greatest gift of all

```
J K J I B H V O O N S K N A H
P E R I S H W Z F E F A S Z E
T O A G P A D L S S T Q Z O I
R B N O H S W O Q V T P N Y N
G N S L M E M A H H I M W E N
M K N I Y N R G D P E P H J T
E A A P W D U L V D X B O R D
V I K V O O R E N F S Z E G E
E E E B R O V O L O E S V L G
R O T H W E C K I G E M E I E
Y C T E I X L M S D G Z R F H
O W N L R L I O L A A W I T L
N P E F E N B O V F V L P E U
E B M K N S A Y M E E E H D T
A Q M G Q Z G L S V D U B C S
```

Moses	believe	Only	send
snake	eternal	Son	condemn
desert	loved	whoever	save
lifted	world	perish	through
everyone	gave	life	him

Bible Memory Verse

For God so loved the world that he gave his one and only Son, that
whoever believes in him shall not perish, but have eternal life.
John 3:16 (NIV)

www.sermon4kids.com

HARVEST CHRISTIAN MINISTRIES

SESSION PLAN

PHASE 2

Instructor: Parent/Guardian	**Date:**
Course Title: God's Word	**Session Number 3**
Unit: Christian Discipleship	

Instructional Objective:
By the end of this session, your child will have a clearer understanding of why the Bible exists and how it relates to their lives. Sessions are designed for ages (3-5), (6-9), (10-12).

Rationale: If children are able to make the connection between an all-knowing and all-powerful God, then they will place a greater value on their individual lives.

Session Content:
    a. Age-appropriate biblically-based sessions outlined in training packet.
    b. Parents and guardians will incorporate sessions from packet which addresses their child's spiritual, emotional, cognitive, and physical needs.

Instructional Procedures:
1. Parent or guardian will open a Bible to Psalms 119:105 and together read the Scripture passage aloud with child.
2. Parent or guardian will light a candle or turn on a flashlight and move to dark area of home in order for child to see the light illuminating the words of Scripture.
3. Parent or guardian will hand out copies of the song, "The Bible is God's word," and sing together. They will also assist child in coloring age-appropriate pictures.

    Closure: Close with a group prayer.

    Materials needed: Holy Bible, handouts, flashlight, voices

PARENT TEACHING GUIDE

SESSION TOPIC

GOD'S WORD

STEP 1: • **Set a time for lesson**	**STEP 2:** • **Pick a place**
STEP 3: • **Have supplies on hand. Holy Bible, handouts, flashlight or candle**	**STEP 4:** • **Open Bible to Psalm 119:105 and read verse together.**
STEP 5: • **Share definition of the Bible and share basic Bible facts** **<u>BEGIN ACTIVITY</u>** 1. **Using a copy of the Bible, go into a dark room and allow light from candle or flashlight to shine on the Bible.** 2 **Hand out copies of the Bible song and sing together.**	**<u>END ACTIVITY</u>** 3. **Assist children in coloring age-appropriate pictures. Share personal stories about our Bible and point out a favorite Scripture passage.**

PARENT TEACHING GUIDE

Daily Log

Date:	Time:
Length of session:	Number of children participants:
Personal Observations: Signature:	Is follow-up needed?

God's Word

Scripture highlight:

Your word is a lamp to my feet and a light for my path. *Psalms 119:105*

What is the Bible? (3-5) (6-9)

The Bible is like a small library made up of 66 books. It has two big sections: the Old Testament and the New Testament. The Old Testament has 39 books, and the New Testament has 27 books. In these 66 books, you will find a total of 1,189 chapters containing about 31,273 verses.

Who wrote the Bible? (10-12)

The words in the Bible came from God. That's why it is called "God's word." God used people to write down the ideas, thoughts, teachings, and words that he wanted to put in the Bible. These people wrote in their own style and in their own language, but they wrote God's word.

Family Activity: (All Ages)

Talk to your children about how God's word should be a guide for living, sort of like a map. Take them to a dark place in your home or outside at night and open your Bible. Using a flashlight or candle, have them use the light source to highlight the words. Then have them to use the light source to guide a few of their steps. Share a family song about God's word.

Ages (3-5) (6-9)

God's word is a lamp

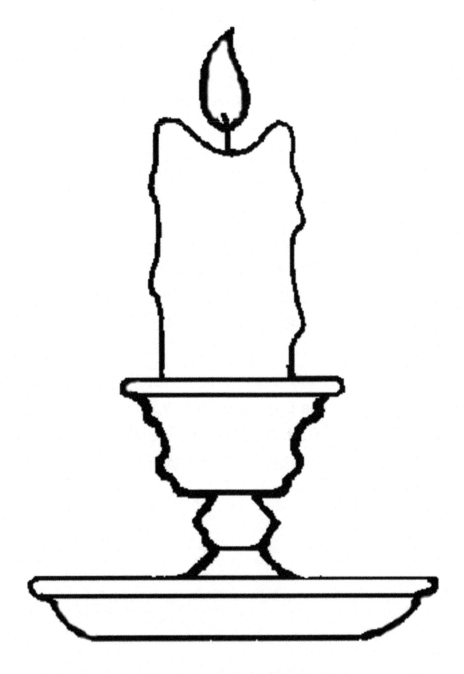

www.sermon4kids.com

(All Ages)
The Bible is God's Word
To the tune of "The Farmer in the Dell"

The Bible is God's Word
The Bible is God's Word
It tells us God loves us
The Bible is God's Word

The Bible is God's Word
The Bible is God's Word
I like to hear God's Word
The Bible is God's Word

The Bible is God's Word
The Bible is God's Word
I like to learn God's Word
The Bible is God's Word

http://dltk-bible.com/bible_is_god.htm

HARVEST CHRISTIAN MINISTRIES

SESSION PLAN

PHASE 2

Instructor: Parent/Guardian	**Date:**
Course Title: God's Love	**Session Number 4**
Unit: Christian Discipleship	

Instructional Objective:
By the end of this session, your child will have a clearer understanding of why God loves them. Sessions are designed for ages (3-5), (6-9), (10-12).

Rationale: If children are able to make the connection between an all-knowing and all-powerful God, then they will place a greater value on their individual lives.

Session Content:
    a. Age-appropriate biblically-based lessons outlined in training packet.
    b. Parents and guardians will incorporate sessions which will address their child's spiritual, cognitive, emotional, and physical needs.

Instructional Procedures:
    1. Parent or guardian will open a Bible to Romans 5:8 and together read the Scripture passage aloud with child.
    2. Parent or guardian will peel off heart sticker and ask each person to place sticker somewhere on their body, preferably at the area of their own heart.
    3. Parent or guardian will hand out copies of the song, "Jesus loves me." Once song has been completed, each person will embrace the other and say, "I love you," and discuss why. Assist child in coloring age-appropriate picture and completing a word search.

    Closure: Close with a group prayer.

      Materials needed: Holy Bible, handouts, heart stickers

PARENT TEACHING GUIDE

LESSON TOPIC

GOD'S LOVE

STEP 1: • Set a time for lesson	**STEP 2:** • Pick a place
STEP 3: • Have supplies on hand. Holy Bible, handouts, coloring crayons	**STEP 4:** • Open Bible to Romans 5:8 and read verse together.
STEP 5: • Share definition of love and how it relates to God. <u>BEGIN ACTIVITY</u> 1. Allow child to peel away heart sticker and give to each member of the family. 2. Handout copies of love songs and sing together.	<u>END ACTIVITY</u> 3. Assist children in coloring age-appropriate pictures, puzzles and word searchers. Embrace each member of the family and share, "I love you."

PARENT TEACHING GUIDE

Daily Log

Date:	Time:
Length of session:	Number of children participants:
Personal Observations Signature: _____	Is follow-up needed?

God's Love

Scripture highlight:

But God demonstrates his own love for us in this: While we were still sinners, Christ died for us. *Romans 5:8*

What is the Love? (6-9)

God is love. The better we get to know God, the better we will understand what true love is all about.

How did God show his love to us? (10-12)

When he sent Jesus to die for our sins, the things we have done wrong.

How can I demonstrate love? (6-9) (10-12)

We should love others, too. Real love is helping others when they need it.

Family Activity: (All Ages)

Give each member of the family a heart sticker and say to them, "I love you." Then explain why you love that person. Parents should share with children why it is important to love each other, especially family members. Group can sing together the song, "Jesus Loves Me."

(All Ages)

Jesus Loves Me

Jesus Loves Me! This I know,
For the Bible tells me so.
Little ones to Him belong;
They are weak, but He is strong.

Yes, Jesus Loves Me!
Yes, Jesus Loves Me!
Yes, Jesus Loves Me!
The Bible tells me so.

Jesus Loves Me still today,
Walking with me on my way,
Wanting as a friend to give
Light and love to all who live.

Refrain

Jesus Loves Me! He who died
Heaven's gate to open wide;
He will wash away my sin,
Let His little child come in.

Refrain

Jesus Loves Me! He will stay
Close beside me all the way;
Thou hast bled and died for me,
I will henceforth live for Thee.

Refrain

www.kididdles.com/lyrics/

Ages (3-5) (6-9)

Jesus died for us

©GospelGifs

Ages (6-9) (10-12)

The Greatest Commandment

Matthew 22:34–40 (NIV)

```
C O M M A N D M E N T G X V T
M H S E C O N D X R L A W D S
M I N D V F L L O Q G V R E X
E T L C H U V B L N R Y E U B
V U O X O B H J I M R S J P I
G O L S S G X R Z N I M W C Z
Q R A O I H A Y O R A Q D A R
T X E E R E A Z A G H U M Y A
L D N A H D H H T W V E J O B
R O O P T R P R I I D S E U P
D G V T X E A X I O L T S R R
A Q X E H E S M X U A I U S G
T U S L H L F T B R I O S E C
Z Q P Z M E X P E R T N W L B
M R O J R B W J A Y I U O F I
```

hearing	Law	Love	mind
Jesus	question	Lord	second
Pharisees	greatest	heart	neighbor
expert	commandment	soul	yourself

Bible Memory Verse

Jesus replied: "Love the Lord your God with all your heart and with all your soul and with all your mind.' This is the first and greatest commandment. And the second is like it: 'Love your neighbor as yourself.'"
Matthew 22:37–39 (NIV)

Sermon4kids.com

HARVEST CHRISTIAN MINISTRIES

SESSION PLAN

PHASE 2

Instructor: Parent/Guardian	**Date:**
Course Title: God's Miracles	**Session Number 5**
Unit: Christian Discipleship	

Instructional Objective:
By the end of this session, your child will have a clearer understanding of the power of God on earth and in heaven. Sessions are designed for ages (3-5), (6-9), (10-12).

Rationale: If children are able to make the connection between an all-knowing and all-powerful God, then they will place a greater value on their individual lives.

Lesson Content:
  a. Age-appropriate biblically-based sessions outlined in training packet.
  b. Parents and guardians will incorporate sessions which will address their child's spiritual, cognitive, emotional, and physical needs.

Instructional Procedures:
  1. Parent or guardian will open a Bible to Matthew 14:19–20 and together read the Scripture passage aloud with child.
  2. Parent or guardian will place cooked fish and bread at the center of the lunch or dinner table. Christ took the contents of the little boy's lunch in order to perform a miracle.
  3. Parent or guardian will share a personal miracle story and allow the child to do the same. At the end of each session, child will receive assistance from parent or guardian in coloring age-appropriate pictures and completing a word search or puzzle.

  Closure: Close with a group prayer.

  Materials needed: Holy Bible, handouts, fish, bread

PARENT TEACHING GUIDE

SESSION TOPIC

GOD'S MIRACLES

STEP 1: • Set a time for lesson	STEP 2: • Pick a place
STEP 3: • Have supplies on hand. Holy Bible, handouts, coloring crayons	STEP 4: • Open Bible to Matthew 14:19-20 and read verses.
STEP 5: • Share lesson during meal **BEGIN ACTIVITY** 1. Locate a place in which you and your children can share a meal which includes fish and bread. Make reference to God's miracle.	**MIRACLE** 1. A supernatural and real event directed by God and performed through His Son Jesus Christ. **END ACTIVITY** 2. Assist children in drawing pictures and completing word puzzles. 3. Share a closing prayer and mention other instances of God's miracles in your own life.

PARENT TEACHING GUIDE

Daily Log

Date:	Time:
Length of session:	Number of children participants:
Personal Observations: Signature: _____	Is follow-up needed?

God's Miracles

Scripture highlight:

"And he directed the people to sit down on the grass. Taking the five loaves of bread and two fish and looking up to heaven, he gave thanks and broke the loaves. Then he gave them to the disciples, and the disciples gave them to the people." *Matthew 14:19–20.*

What is a miracle? (6-9) (10-12)

A miracle is a supernatural and real event directed by God and performed through his son Jesus Christ.

Jesus Christ performed more than 40 Miracles in the Bible. (3-5) (6-9)

The Scripture passage explains one of those miracles involving a little boy.

Family Activity (All Ages)

At lunch or dinner, place fish and bread on the family menu. During time together at the table, share with children how Jesus took a little boy's lunch and multiplied it to feed 5,000 people. Emphasize that Jesus took the bread and broke it. You should also break bread, and, like Christ, pray over meal. Share one of your own miracle stories of how Jesus worked a miracle through multiplying something in your life or the family's' life.

Ages (3-5) (6-9)

www.sermon4kids.com

Ages (10-12)

Feeding the 5000

```
C J A C H N T U K Z T G U U S
P O J K P B W U A B A H E E U
J Z C S L R E V X J Q E Z N T
E I B A A I L V W X G A X L B
S L A T N P V R O L L U N E
V L S I D N E Z U C N E W Z S
J O K S E H B G G V A D E D O
F A E F D X N L F J W L W T D
O V T I B H F I S H P O A T B
L E F E H W L F Y O R O V H E
L S U D J P Q M E C B J H A Q
O O L E S Z X P J L S M D N X
W Z S J E S U S L E I E X K V
E U E Z O S D D H F I F J S E
D D T O W N S P W T B R Q B X
```

Boat	landed	loaves	satisfied
crowds	Jesus	fish	twelve
followed	healed	thanks	basketfuls
towns	sick	people	left

They all ate and were satisfied, and the disciples picked up
twelve basketfuls of broken pieces that were left over.
Matthew 14:20 (NIV)

www.sermons4kids.com

Phase Two Timeline/Session outline

MY BELIEFS	MY PRAYER	MY PARENTS	MY CHURCH- MY PASTOR	BAPTISM- COMMUNION
Scripture: Romans 10:9 Facilitator: Parent Allotted time: 1 hour	Scripture: Matthew 6:9–13 Facilitator: Parent Allotted time: 1 hour	Scripture: Genesis 6:14–16 Ephesians 6:1-3 Facilitator: Parent Allotted time: 1 hour	Scripture: Matthew 16:13, Ephesians 4:11 Facilitator: Parent Allotted time: 1 hour	Scripture: Matthew 3:13–16 Matthew 26:26–28 Facilitator: Parent Allotted time: 1 hour
Activity: Explain the importance of belief in God and his Son Jesus Christ. Have children engage in age appropriate family activity about things they believe.	Activity: Pray together the Lord's prayer in a familiar place within the home. Permit child to say their own prayers to God. Have child complete prayer handout	Activity: Discuss the importance of fol-lowing directions using a house-hold cooking item. Also, share the example of Noah obeying God.	Activity: Explain that church is made up of people who believe in Jesus. Identify church location Explain how a pastor is like a shepherd guard-ing sheep	Activity: Define baptism and how John baptized Jesus. Define Holy Com-munion and ex-plain immersion. Use bread and grape juice to ex-plain communion
Materials: 1 Items which will stimulate 5 senses. 2. Prayer of Salvation hand-out 3. Bible name word search	Materials: 1. Coloring hand-out 2. Prayer quiz	Materials: 1. Household food item 2. Noah word search 3. Ark coloring page	Materials: 1.Work search 2.Shepherd/ sheep coloring	Materials: 1 Word search Baptism. Holy communion 2. Coloring page

HARVEST CHRISTIAN MINISTRIES

SESSION PLAN

PHASE 2

Instructor: Parent/Guardian	Date:
Course Title: My beliefs	Session Number 6
Unit: Christian Discipleship	

Instructional Objective:
By the end of this session, your child will have a clearer understanding of their belief in God. Sessions are designed for ages (3-5), (6-9), (10-12).

Rationale: If children are able to make the connection between an all-knowing and all-powerful God, then they will place a greater value on their individual lives.

Lesson Content:

   A. Age-appropriate biblically-based sessions outlined in training packet.
   B. Parents and guardians will incorporate sessions which will address their child's spiritual, cognitive, emotional, and physical needs.

Instructional Procedures:

1. Parent or guardian will open a Bible to Romans 10:9 and together read Scripture aloud with child.
2. Parent or guardian will assemble items on flat surface and using their five senses, assist child in identifying each one. The parents' goal is to help child identify with things they cannot physically see but believe exist.
3. At the end of session, child will receive assistance from parent or guardian in coloring age-appropriate pictures and completing a word search or puzzle.

Closure: Close with a group prayer.

Materials needed: Holy Bible, handouts, household items

PARENT TEACHING GUIDE

SESSION TOPIC

MY BELIEFS

STEP 1: • Set a time for lesson 	STEP 2: • Pick a place
STEP 3: • Have supplies on hand. Holy Bible, household edible items such as favorite fruit or snack, coloring crayons 	STEP 4: • Open Bible to Romans 10:9-10 And read verse.
STEP 5: BEGIN ACTIVITY 1. Locate edible items within your home, such as your child's favorite snack or fruit. 2. Assist children in believing what they can't see with the natural eye but recognize by other means, such as taste or smell.	STEP 6: END ACTIVITY Assist children in drawing pictures and completing word puzzles.

PARENT TEACHING GUIDE

Daily Log

Date:	Time:
Length of session:	Number of children participants:
Personal Observations: Signature: _____	Is follow up needed?

My beliefs

Scripture highlight:

"Say with your mouth, "Jesus is Lord." Believe in your heart that God raised him from the dead. Then you will be saved." *Romans 10:9 (NIRV)*

How do you get Jesus in your heart? (3-5)

The heart is located inside the body and is responsible for keeping us alive. Just like the physical heart, there is a spiritual heart. That "heart" is deep down inside us—where we really feel and believe. We can receive Jesus in our spiritual heart by asking Him to come in.

How can Jesus fit in my heart? (6-9)

When someone says, "Jesus lives in my heart," the person means that he has asked Jesus to be his Savior—to forgive and take care of him or her—and that Jesus is in charge of his or her life. When someone asks Jesus to take over, God really does come inside—the Holy Spirit comes and lives inside that person.

Family Activity (All Ages)

We believe in things we cannot always see. In this activity, child will engage each of their five senses. In each instance, child's eyes must be closed.

1. Have children take a bite from their favorite food and then ask them to identify the food and open their eyes.

2. Have children hear a favorite song played from a piece of electronic equipment, then have them to follow the sound to where it is located.

3. Have children touch something familiar within the home, such as a favorite toy or household object such as an eating utensil and identify it before opening their eyes.

4. Have children smell something familiar fruit like an orange and identify it before opening their eyes.

5. After each individual activity, have the child to open his or her eyes and make a visual connection with each object he or she has been asked to identify.

Ages (6-9) (10-12)

DO YOU BELIEVE?

Do you believe the moon has rocks?
Do you believe man landed on the moon?

Why or why not?

When you see a gift under the Christmas tree with you name on it, do you believe there is something nice inside?

Why or why not?

Do you believe you have a heart inside your body?
Do you believe it is the right size?

Why or why not?

"We believe many things even though we cannot see them. We believe there are rocks on the moon even though we have never been to the moon. We believe there are nice things inside wrapped presents, even though we cannot tell for sure until we open the box. We believe we have a heart, and it is the right size although we have never actually seen our heart. Although we cannot see God, we believe He is real and that He loves us. In fact, He loves us so much He gave His only begotten Son, that whosoever believes in Him will not perish but have everlasting life. (John 3:16) Believing is the first step to real salvation.

Do you believe?"

Ages (6-9) (10-12)

Dear Lord Jesus, I admit that I am a _____ and have been disobedient to you. I am truly sorry and I ask for your _____. I believe you are the _____ of God and that you died on the cross to save me. I believe you rose again and you are alive, and you hear my _____. I ask you now to come into my _____ and take control of my life. I ask you to be my Lord and Savior. Amen

HEART   PRAYERS   SON   SINNER   FORGIVENESS

www.sermon4kids.com

HARVEST CHRISTIAN MINISTRIES

SESSION PLAN

PHASE 2

Instructor: Parent/Guardian	**Date:**
Course Title: My Prayer	**Session Number 7**
Unit: Christian Discipleship	

Instructional Objective:
By the end of this session, your child will have a clearer understanding of prayer and what it means to pray to God. Sessions are designed for ages (3-5), (6-9), (10-12).

Rationale: If children are able to make the connection between an all-knowing and all-powerful God, then they will place a greater value on their individual lives.

Lesson Content:
    a. Age-appropriate biblically-based sessions outlined in training packet.
    b. Parents and guardians will incorporate lessons which will address their child's spiritual, cognitive, emotional, and physical needs.

Instructional Procedures:
    1. Parent or guardian will open a Bible to Matthew 6:9–13 and together read the Scripture passage aloud with child.
    2. Parent or guardian will assemble family and kneel on their knees in a location within the home. They will press their hands together with each finger touching the other. They'll be asked to close their eyes and take turn saying a prayer. Parent or guardian can begin the activity.
    3. Parent or guardian will share the answers to prayers they have prayed and ask the child to do the same. At the end of session, child will receive assistance from parent or guardian in coloring age-appropriate pictures and completing a word search or puzzle.

Closure: Close with a group prayer.

    Materials needed: Holy Bible, handouts

PARENT TEACHING GUIDE

SESSION TOPIC

MY PRAYER

STEP 1:	STEP 2:
• **Set a time for lesson**	• **Pick a place**
STEP 3:	STEP 4:
• **Have supplies on hand. Holy Bible, handouts, coloring crayons** 	• **Open Bible to Matthew 6:9-13 and read verses.**
STEP 5:	PRAY
• **Share with child why you pray.** **BEGIN ACTIVITY** 1. **Assemble family and find a location in which you can all bow on your knees and take turn saying a prayer.** 2. **Assist child in understanding how prayer has been beneficial in your life.**	• **To talk or have a conversation with God** **END ACTIVITY** 3. **Assist children in drawing pictures and completing word puzzles.** 4. **Have child help decide on when the family will pray again as a group.**

PARENT TEACHING GUIDE

Daily Log

Date:	Time:
Length of session:	Number of children participants:
Personal Observations: Signature: _____	Is follow up needed?

My Prayer

Scripture highlight (All Ages)

9"This, then, is how you should pray: 'Our Father in heaven, hallowed be your name, 10your kingdom come, your will be done on earth as it is in heaven. 11Give us today our daily bread. 12Forgive us our debts, as we also have forgiven our debtors. 13And lead us not into temptation, but deliver us from the evil one." *Matthew 6:9–13*

Why do we prayer? (All Ages)

Prayer is talking with God. When we have a good friend, we talk to that person about all sorts of things. That's part of being a friend. In the same way, we should talk to God about what is happening in our life. God wants us to share our life with him, to tell him about what makes us happy, sad, and afraid. He wants to know what we want and what we would like him to do, for ourselves and for others. Also, when we pray, we open ourselves up to God so that he can make good changes in us.

How can God hear everyone's prayer at once? (All Ages)

God can hear everyone's prayers at once because God is everywhere. We can only be at one place at a time, and usually we can't understand more than one person at a time. But God is not like us—he is not limited. Not only can God hear and understand everyone who is praying to him in many different languages, but he also can give each person his full attention. Isn't that great?

Family Activity (All Ages)

Parent or guardian will assemble family and kneel in a location within the home. They will press their hands together with each finger touching the other. They'll be asked to close their eyes and take turns saying a prayer. Parent or guardian can begin the activity. Share with your child an instance when God answered your prayer. Have the child to share a similar testimony.

Ages (3-5) (6-9)

www.sermon4kids.com

Ages (6-9) (10-12)

Prayer

Four prayers God will answer

1. God, at school help me to_____

2. God, help me to _____ my parents.

3. God, help me to _____ to my brothers and sisters

4. God, help me to _____ when I play with my friends

A. Obey   **B. Be kind**   **C. Study hard**   **D. Take turns**

www.sermon4kids.com

HARVEST CHRISTIAN MINISTRIES

SESSION PLAN

PHASE 2

Instructor: Parent/Guardian	**Date:**
Course Title: My Parents	**Session Number 8**
Unit: Christian Discipleship	

Instructional Objective:
By the end of this session, your child will have a clearer understanding of why it is important to obey God and their parents. Sessions are designed for ages (3-5), (6-9), (10-12).

Rationale: If children are able to make the connection between an all-knowing and all-powerful God, then they will place a greater value on their individual lives.

Lesson Content:

    A. Age-appropriate biblically-based sessions outlined in training packet.
    B. Parents and guardians will incorporate sessions which will address their child's spiritual, cognitive, emotional, and physical needs.

Instructional Procedures:

    1. Parent or guardian will open a Bible to Ephesians 6:1–3 and Genesis 6:14–16 and together read passages aloud with child.
    2. Parent or guardian will assemble the family and display cooking instructions for a food item and explain why it is important to follow each step.
    3. Parent or guardian will share why they should follow God's instructions in their own lives and that those instructions are found in the Bible. Genesis 6:14-16 and the story of Noah can be used as an example. At the end of session, child will receive assistance from parent or guardian in coloring age-appropriate pictures and completing a word search or puzzle.

    Closure: Close with a group prayer.

    Materials needed: Holy Bible, handouts, household cooking item

PARENT TEACHING GUIDE

SESSION TOPIC

MY PARENTS

STEP 1:	STEP 2:
• Set a time for lesson 	• Pick a place
STEP 3: • Have supplies on hand. Household cooking items, toy boat, Bible, handouts, and coloring crayons 	**STEP 4:** • Open Bible to Ephesians 6:1–3, Genesis 6:14–16 and read verses.
STEP 5: • Share definition of parent **BEGIN ACTIVITY** 1. Assemble family and display cooking instructions for a food item. Point out importance of carefully following each direction. 2. Have child assist you in reading and following cooking instructions.	**PARENT** • Those responsible for caring and providing for you **END ACTIVITY** Assist children in drawing pictures and completing word puzzles.

PARENT TEACHING GUIDE

Daily Log

Date:	Time:
Length of session:	Number of children participants:
Personal Observations:	Is follow-up needed?
Signature:	

My Parents

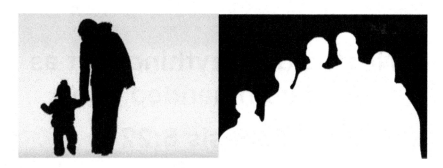

Scripture highlight:

[1]Children, obey your parents in the Lord, for this is right. [2]"Honor your father and mother"—which is the first commandment with a promise— [3]"that it may go well with you and that you may enjoy long life on the earth." *Ephesians 6:1–3*

So make yourself an ark of cypress wood; make rooms in it and coat it with pitch inside and out. [15] This is how you are to build it: The ark is to be 450 feet long, 75 feet wide and 45 feet high. [16] Make a roof for it and finish [c] the ark to within 18 inches of the top. Put a door in the side of the ark and make lower, middle and upper decks. *Genesis 6:14–16*

Why do I need to obey my parents? (All Ages)

We need to obey our parents because it is what God tells us to do in the Bible. God smiles when we do what our parents instruct us to do. It is right.

Why do our parents ask us to obey them? (All Ages)

Our parents ask us to obey them because they love us. God loves us. He is our heavenly parent, and we are taught obey him.

Family Activity (All Ages)

Parent or guardian will assemble the family and display cooking instructions for a food item and explain why it is important to follow each step. Allow the child to see how his or her favorite meal is prepared using explicit instructions.

Ages (3-5) (6-9)

Noah did everything just as God commanded him.

Genesis 6:22

Ages (6-9) (10-12)

Noah and the Ark

Noah did everything just as God commanded him.
Genesis 6:22 (NIV)

Based on Genesis 6:9-22; 7:24; 8:14-19 (NIV)

```
P B L A M E L E S S Z C M I F
A F V Z H Y F H H O Y Y N I I
V I R C N O A H M O A P H R I
I Z F P P C V M W O W R D O P
O P R E L O A R K Z U E P O Y
L R J O W H G A P H F S G M D
E C W P H X L W U I D S S S E
N R K L D E C K S E T H L O S
C E R E N D E B F A T C O B T
E A O A W J Q I I R Q A H U R
L T O I S W W W A R Y N D I O
U U F X O T O E B E D I T L Y
F R S F N Q V O K W A M F D D
L E B T S J F K D X S A B T K
V S R I G H T E O U S L J I T
```

BLAMELESS	SONS	CREATURES	DECKS	PITCH
BUILD	PEOPLE	ANIMAL	ARK	EARTH
WOOD	DESTROY	ROOF	VIOLENCE	ROOMS
RIGHTEOUS	WIFE	CYPRESS	BIRD	NOAH

www.sermon4kids.com

HARVEST CHRISTIAN MINISTRIES

SESSION PLAN

PHASE 2

Instructor: Parent/Guardian	**Date:**
Course Title: My Church, My Pastor	**Session Number 9**
Unit: Christian Discipleship	

Instructional Objective:
By the end of this session, your child will have a clearer understanding of the difference between the church as a body of Christ and the pastor as shepherd of the flock. Sessions are designed for ages (3-5), (6-9), (10-12).

Rationale: If children are able to make the connection between an all-knowing and all-powerful God, then they will place a greater value on their individual lives.

Lesson Content:
   A. Age-appropriate biblically-based sessions outlined in training packet.
   B. Parents and guardians will incorporate sessions which will address their child's spiritual, cognitive, emotional, and physical needs.

Instructional Procedures:
   1. Parent or guardian will open a Bible to Matthew 16:18 and Ephesians 4:11 and together read passages aloud with child.
   2. Parent or guardian will observe a handout which makes the connection between a church and school, a shepherd and a pastor.
   3. Parent or guardian will talk about the duties of the pastor at Harvest and discuss his role each and every Sunday morning and how he feeds the people like a shepherd would feed his flock. At the end of session, child will receive assistance from parent or guardian in coloring age-appropriate pictures and completing a word search or puzzle.

Closure: Close with a group prayer.

Materials needed: Holy Bible, handouts

PARENT TEACHING GUIDE

SESSION TOPIC

MY CHURCH-MY PASTOR

STEP 1: • Set a time for lesson 	STEP 2: • Pick a place
STEP 3: • Have supplies on hand. Holy Bible, handouts, and coloring crayons	STEP 4: • Open Bible to Matthew 16:18, Ephesians 4:11
STEP 5: • Share definition of Church-Pastor **BEGIN ACTIVITY** 1. Use handout pictures to help child understand the differences and similarities between the pastor and teacher, church and school. 2. Assist children in understanding the difference by sharing the name of your church and the name of your pastor.	CHURCH • A group of people who believe in Jesus Christ and who meeting regular to pray, sing, and spend time together PASTOR 3. Person appointed to lead the church to meet the spiritual needs of the people END ACTIVITY 4. Assist children in drawing pictures and completing word puzzles.

PARENT TEACHING GUIDE

Daily Log

Date:	Time:
Length of session:	Number of children participants:
Personal Observations: Signature: _____	Is follow-up needed?

My Church-My Pastor

Scripture highlight:

[18]And I say also unto thee, That thou art Peter, and upon this rock I will build my church; and the gates of hell shall not prevail against it" *Matthew 16:18*

[11]And he gave some, apostles; and some, prophets; and some, evangelists; and some, pastors and teachers; *Ephesians 4:11*

What is the Christian Church? (All Ages)

A group of people who believe in Jesus Christ and that he is the Son of God and that he was crucified, but rose from the dead. Church is a community.

Who is the Pastor? (All Ages)

The man or woman appointed to lead people in the church based on what the Bible says. He preaches, visits the sick, prays with people, and teaches children and their parents what the Bible says is right. He is referred to as a shepherd.

Why is he called the shepherd? (All Ages)

He is called a shepherd because he takes care of the sheep, which are the people in his church. He watches over them and tells them about right and wrong, based on what is in the Bible.

Family Activity: (All Ages)

Parent or guardian will help child compare the surroundings at his school and those at the church. The school is a place where children learn about subjects like reading, writing, and math. Parents and guardians will then, on a second handout, Explain how the church is the place where people learn about God, Jesus, and love. A final handout will help parents and guardians make a connection between a shepherd whose job it is to look after a sheep with his rod and staff and the job of a pastor whose job it is to teach the people with the Bible.

MY SCHOOL

- **READING**

- **WRITING**

- **MATH**

Ages (3-5) (6-9)

Jesus and Lamb

For more coloring pages, visit
www.childrensstorybooksonline.com

Ages (10-12)

The Good Shepherd

John 10:11-18 (NIV)

ACROSS

1. Wild animal that looks like a dog and hunts in packs

3. The period from birth to death

5. A strong feeling of affection

6. Goes faster than walking

9. What we use to speak

11. One who takes care of the sheep

DOWN

2. The male parent

3. To hear or pay attention to something

4. A group of sheep herded together

7. Wooly animals which are similar to goats

8. The opposite of bad

10. A small place where animals are kept

Words Used			
good	sheep	runs	listen
shepherd	wolf	father	pen
life	flock	voice	love

www.sermon4kids.com

HARVEST CHRISTIAN MINISTRIES

SESSION PLAN

PHASE 2

Instructor: Parent/Guardian	**Date:**
Course Title: Baptism-Communion	**Session Number 10**
Unit: Christian Discipleship	

Instructional Objective:
By the end of this session your child will have a clearer understanding of the importance of Baptism and Communion and why they are important to Christians. Sessions are designed for ages (3-5), (6-9), (10-12).

Rationale: If children are able to make the connection between an all-knowing and all-powerful God, then they will place a greater value on their individual lives.

Lesson Content:
A. Age-appropriate biblically-based sessions outlined in training packet.
B. Parents and guardians will incorporate lessons which will address their child's spiritual, cognitive, emotional, and physical needs.

Instructional Procedures:
1. Parent or guardian will open a Bible to Matthew 3:13–14 and Matthew 26:26–28 and together read passages aloud with child.
2. Parent or guardian will assemble family and display handouts, a container of grape juice, and a slice of bread in the center of the table.
3. Parent or guardian will use handouts of familiar community symbols to help explain how religious symbols can help us remember the life and the ministry of Jesus Christ. A container of grape juice will be used to talk about how it is symbol for the blood Jesus shed for our sins. A piece of bread will help explain how Jesus' body was broken for us on the cross. At the end of session, child will receive assistance from parent or guardian in coloring age appropriate pictures and completing a word search or puzzle.

Closure: Close with a group prayer.

Materials needed: Holy Bible, handouts, juice, and bread

PARENT TEACHING GUIDE

SESSION TOPIC

BAPTISM-COMMUNION

STEP 1: • **Set a time for lesson** 	**STEP 2:** • **Pick a place**
STEP 3: • **Have supplies on hand. Juice, bread, Bible, handouts, camera, coloring crayons** 	**STEP 4:** • **Open Bible to Matthew 3:13–14, Matthew 26:26–28 and read verses.**
STEP 5: • **Share definition of Baptism and Communion** **BEGIN ACTIVITY** 1. **Locate a place** 2. **Assist children in taking pictures of what they see**	**BAPTISM** • **To put or go under water as a symbol of new life in Jesus Christ.** **COMMUNION** • **Sharing of juice (wine) and bread as a symbol of Jesus death and resurrection** **END ACTIVITY** **Assist children in drawing pictures and completing word puzzles.**

PARENT TEACHING GUIDE

Daily Log

Date:	Time:
Length of session:	Number of children participants:
Personal Observations: Signature: _____	Is follow up needed?

Baptism-Communion

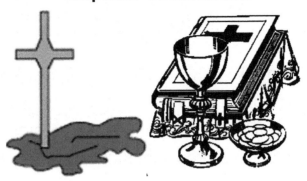

Scripture highlight:

[13]Then Jesus came from Galilee to the Jordan to be baptized by John. [14]But John tried to deter him, saying, "I need to be baptized by you, and do you come to me?" *Matthew 3:13–14*

[26]While they were eating, Jesus took bread, gave thanks and broke it, and gave it to his disciples, saying, "Take and eat; this is my body." [27]Then he took the cup, gave thanks and offered it to them, saying, "Drink from it, all of you. [28]This is my blood of the[a] covenant, which is poured out for many for the forgiveness of sins. *Matthew 26:26–28.*

What is Baptism? (6-9)(10-12)

Baptize means to put or go under water. It is a symbol of new life in Jesus Christ. When we are baptized, it is a picture of what Jesus has done for us. He died, was buried, and rose again to wash away our sin and give us a new life in him.

What is Communion (Lord's Supper)? (10-12)

Communion is also a symbol of new life in Jesus Christ. Bread is **a symbol** of His body. The juice is of His blood. He left behind a picture for us to remember him by. It isn't a picture in an album that we can look at and remember what Jesus looked like, but it is a picture to help us remember what Jesus did for us. We call it "The Lord's Supper.

Family Activity: (All Ages)

For Baptism, identify pictures of symbols in your community, such as a favorite place to eat, a traffic light, or a familiar school sign. Assist the children in sharing what each symbol represents. In the same way, being baptized is symbol of a changed or new life in Christ. In order to discuss the ordinance of Communion, use a container of grape juice and a piece of bread, to try and make the connection between how the juice is a symbol for the blood Jesus shed for our sins on the cross. Likewise, the bread will be used to help explain how Jesus' body was broken for us.

SYMBOLS

Help your child identify the symbols below and what they represent.

---

http://www.mcdonalds.com/

Ages (3-5) (6-9)

www.sermon4kids.com

Ages (10-12)

The Baptism of Jesus

One day when the crowds were being baptized, Jesus himself was baptized. Luke 3:21 (NIV)

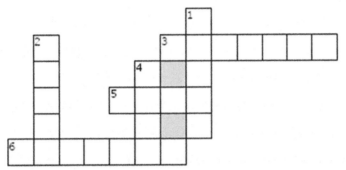

ACROSS

3. Shoes that are fastened to the foot by straps.
5. The Holy Spirit came down from heaven in the form of a _____.
6. When Jesus prayed, the _____ opened.

DOWN

1. The liquid that John used to baptize people.
2. What was heard when Jesus was baptized.
4. The name of the man who baptized Jesus.

John	voice	water
dove	sandals	heavens

www.sermon4kids.com

Ages (3-5) (6-9)

www.sermon4kids.com

APPENDIX C
SESSION PICTURES

Participants in Session two

Participant children during session four

BIBLIOGRAPHY

Allen, Holley Catterson. *Nurturing Children's Spirituality, Christian Perspectives and Best Practices.* Eugene, OR: Cascade Books, 2008.

Anderson, Herbert and Johnson, B.W. Susan. *Regarding Children, a new perspective for Childhood and families.* Louisville, KY: Westminster John Knox Press, 1994.

Baltimore County Government, 2007:http://www.co.ba.md.us/ (accessed on May 30, 2008).

Barna, George. *Transforming Children into Spiritual Champions: Why children should Be your church's #1 priority,* Regal: Ventura California, 2003.

Bickimer, David Arthur. *Leadership in Religious Education,* Religious Education Press: Birmingham, Alabama, 1989.

http://www.biblos.com/

Bunge, Marcia. *The Child in Christian Thought,* Grand Rapids MI: William B. Eerdmans Publishing Company, 2001.

Carson, Ben. *Take the Risk*, Grand Rapids, Michigan: Zondervan, 2008.

Carter, Harold A. *America where are you Going,* Gateway Press, Inc. Baltimore MD, 1994.

www.childrensstorybooksonline.com

Children's Ministry Magazine (accessed March 23, 2009)

Cooper, Scott. *God at the Kitchen Table,* New York: Three Rivers Press, 2002.

Ferguson, Everett. *Backgrounds of Early Christianity*, Grand Rapid, Michigan: William B. Eerdmans Publishing Company, 1993.

Fosarelli, Pat D. *A.S.A.P Ages, Stages, and Phases from Infancy to Adolescence,* Liguori MO: Liguori, 2006.

Galindo, Israel The *Craft of Christian Teaching: Essentials For Becoming a Very Good Teacher,* Judson Press: Valley Forge, PA 1998.

Gardner, Howard. *Frames of Mind, the Theory of Multiple Intelligences*, New York: NY BasicBooks, 1983.

Hiscox, Edward T. *The Hiscox Standard Baptist Manual*, Valley Forge, PA: Judson Press, 1965), 81.

Juvenile Offenders and Victims National Report Series, 2006: http://ojjdp. ncirs.org (Accessed on May 30, 2008).

http://kididdles.com/lyrics/j008.html

Krych, Margaret A. *The Ministry of Children's Education: Foundations, Contexts, and Practices*, Minneapolis, MN: Fortress Press, 2004.

Maryland Adolescent Survey, Maryland State Department of Education. 2007: http://www.marylandpublicschools.org/NR rdonlyres/852505C8-7FDB-4E4 E-B34E-448A5E2BE8BC/18944MAS2007FinalReport_revised111808.pdf (accessed on May 30, 2008).

Maryland Youth Risk Behavior Survey, Maryland State Department of Education. 2005: http://www.marylandpublicschools.org. (Accessed on May 30. 2008).

May, Scottie, Posterski, Beth, Stonehouse, Catherine and Cannell, Linda. *Children Matter: Celebrating Their Place in the Church, Family, and Community,* Grand Rapids, Michigan Wm, B. Eerdmans Publishing, 2005.

Moran, Gabriel. *Education Toward Adulthood*, Paulist Press: New York, 1979.

Piaget, Jean and Inhelder, Barbel, *The Psychology of the Child* Basicbooks: New York, 2000.

Perkins, James C. *Building Up Zion's Walls*, Valley Forge PA: Judson Press, 1999.

Perkins, John M. *Restoring At-Risk communities Doing it together and doing it righ* Baker Books Grand Rapids, MI 2008.

Ratcliff, Donald. *Children's Spirituality, Christian Perspectives, Research and Applications,* Eugene Oregon: Cascade Books, 2004.

Sell, Charles M. *Family Ministry: The Enrichment of Family Life through the Church,* Grand Rapids, Michigan: Zondervan Publishing House, 1981.

Singer Dorothy A and Revenson, Tracey A. *"A Piaget Primer How a child thinks."* Penguin Books: New York, 1996.

Spurgeon, C.H. *Spiritual Parenting,* New Kensington PA: Whitaker House, 2003.

The King James Holy Bible

The New International Version Bible

Wilson, Leslie Walker. *Improving Your Elementary School,* New York: Eye on Education, 2007.

Wolpe, David J. *Teaching your Children about God: A Modern Jewish Approach,* New York: Harper Perennial, 1993.

Participant A, "Project Harvest." [Oral Presentation, Harvest Christian Ministries, Baltimore, MD., May 26, 2009].

Participant B "Project Harvest." [Oral Presentation, Harvest Christian Ministries, Baltimore, MD., May 26, 2009].

Participant C, "Project Harvest." [Oral Presentation, Harvest Christian Ministries, Baltimore, MD., May 26, 2009].

Participant D, "Project Harvest." [Oral Presentation, Harvest Christian Ministries, Baltimore, MD., May 26, 2009].

Participant E," [Oral Presentation, Harvest Christian Ministries, Baltimore, MD., May 26, 2009].

Participant F, "Project Harvest." [Oral Presentation, Harvest Christian Ministries, Baltimore, MD., May 26, 2009].

Participant G, "Project Harvest." [Oral Presentation, Harvest Christian Ministries, Baltimore, MD., May 26, 2009].

Participant H, "Project Harvest." [Oral Presentation, Harvest Christian Ministries, Baltimore, MD., May 26, 2009].

Child Participant I, "Project Harvest." [Oral Presentation, Harvest Christian Ministries, Baltimore, MD., May 26, 2009].

Child Participant J," Project Harvest." [Oral Presentation, Harvest Christian Ministries, Baltimore, MD., May 26, 2009].

CPSIA information can be obtained
at www.ICGtesting.com
Printed in the USA
LVOW02s1629080817
544257LV00005B/28/P